THE LIBRARY
ST. MARY'S COLLEGE OF MARYLAND
ST. MARY'S CITY, MARYLAND 20686

Jaishankar Prasad

Twayne's World Authors Series

Leslie Flemming, Editor of Indian Literature
University of Arizona

TWAS 631

Jaishankar Prasad

By Rajendra Singh
Université de Montréal

Twayne Publishers • Boston

Jaishankar Prasad

Rajendra Singh

Copyright © 1982 by G. K. Hall & Company
Published by Twayne Publishers
A Division of G. K. Hall & Company
70 Lincoln Street
Boston, Massachusetts 02111

Book Production by Marne B. Sultz
Book Design by Barbara Anderson

Printed on permanent/durable
acid-free paper and bound in
The United States of America.

Library of Congress Cataloging in Publication Data
Singh, Rajendra, 1943–
    Jaishankar Prasad.

    (Twayne's world authors series; TWAS 631)
    Bibliography: p. 140
    1. Prasad, Jaishankar, 1889–1937—Criticism and
interpretation.   I. Title.   II. Series.
PK2098.P7Z8824   891'.438509   82-903
ISBN 0–8057–6474–7   AACR2

To
 A.C.
 P.S.
 and Graham Greene

Contents

About the Author
Preface
Acknowledgments
Chronology

> *Chapter One*
> The Man, the Place, and the Times   1
>
> *Chapter Two*
> The Early Years   17
>
> *Chapter Three*
> Dramatize, Dramatize, Dramatize   35
>
> *Chapter Four*
> Some More Fiction   51
>
> *Chapter Five*
> The Return to Drama   68
>
> *Chapter Six*
> The Lyric and the Novel Revisited   77
>
> *Chapter Seven*
> The Epic Voice: *Kamayani*   86

Chapter Eight
Postscript   105

Chapter Nine
Conclusion   119

Notes and References   125
Selected Bibliography   140
Index   145

About the Author

Rajendra Singh was born in a small village near Delhi, India. He spent his boyhood days in Banaras, the home-town of Prasad. In 1966 he was awarded a Fulbright Scholarship to study American language and literature in the United States. He found the language part really fascinating and received the Ph.D. in linguistics from Brown University. He is currently associate professor of linguistics at Université de Montréal. Although a linguist by choice, he likes to read and sometimes even write about literature. He has published articles in practically every journal in linguistics and a monograph on E. M. Forster. He is also the editor of a forthcoming book on Sanskrit. His main interests are: English, Hindi, and what he calls "grammars in contact." A naturalized Canadian, he lives, with his wife and two children, in Montréal.

Preface

Jaishankar Prasad (1889–1929), whose life and work I attempt to introduce to the English-speaking world in this book, deserves to be better known than he is. Perhaps the greatest Modern Hindi writer, Prasad has, unfortunately, not been picked up by many translators, possibly because he is a difficult writer to translate.

He deserves to be better known for at least three reasons: (1) he is a great poet and playwright; (2) he is the first major writer of Modern Hindi; and (3) his thematic interests and aesthetic development are likely to be of interest to anyone concerned with modern literature in general and Modern Hindi literature in particular.

One of the first *Chhayavadins* ("Romantics") revolting against the puritanical strictures of the verse-makers and didactic critics of the previous century, Prasad not only accomplished his romantic quest but also went beyond it to achieve the rich complexity of poetic statement rarely accomplished by romantics. A lyricist of the naive and the sentimental, Prasad is also the composer—and I use the term intentionally—of *Kamayani*, the epic effort to express the burdens of the modern psyche in mythological terms rich enough for a Milton and complex enough for a Blake or a Yeats.

He was, however, not only a lyricist and an epic writer but also a playwright—a rare romantic indeed—whose match has yet to appear on the literary stage of Hindi. The artistically rich recreation of the splendor that was India in plays such as *Ajatshatru* and *Chandragupta* achieves the panoramic glitter of a Walter Scott novel and the complexity of a Shakespearean tragedy.

His short stories and one-act plays such as "Mamata," "Madhulika," and *Ek Ghunt* concentrate on those forgotten moments of crisis and conflict that must have shaped the rich and complex fabric of the Indian past. Novelistic in appearance, dramatic in

JAISHANKAR PRASAD

structure and poetic in texture, his short stories are achievements of a rare kind.

A study of Prasad's works and of his growth as an artist from an almost decadent Shelley to a mature dramatist provides a significant insight into the making of a major literary voice of this century.

My interest in introducing the work of Prasad to a wider audience goes back to my undergraduate days when I first read his work with pleasure. Although I decided to go on and study things other than Modern Hindi literature, I always kept a copy of his *Kamayani* with me.

The present book seeks to provide nothing more than an introductory survey of Prasad's work. The plan is rather simple: the first chapter provides a brief outline of Hindi literature and deals with his life and times, the last chapter with a general evaluation of his work and of his contribution to Hindi literature, and the chapters in between provide an introductory account of his work. I have concentrated on his major works. His minor works sometimes get only a mention from me. This may strike some as unfair, but in my effort to introduce his work to a wider audience, I have deliberately decided not to clutter up an introduction such as this with exotic names. Exhaustiveness is not always desirable. It can, as a matter of fact, sometimes be boring.

Since names of works discussed in this book are likely to appear exotic and quaint to my readers, I have adopted the convention of referring to them with their translation equivalents in English, except that when a work is first introduced I provide the original Hindi title in brackets. Thus, although *Kankal* is introduced as *The Skeleton* [*Kankal*], it is discussed as *The Skeleton*. Proper-name titles such as *Chandragupta* have been left alone. Hindi names, however, do have a transparent semantics, and where the meaning of a proper name seems important, it has been provided either in the text itself or in a footnote. Thus the information that *Kamayani* literally means "the daughter of Kama, the Indian God of Love" is available to the reader for it is impor-

Preface

tant for an understanding of the book. In the Chronology also, the original Hindi title appears after its translation equivalent in English. I hope the convention of referring to a work by its English title will make for easier reading. The transliteration of Hindi and Sanskrit names follows the standard practice.

Although I have kept the aim of introducing Prasad's work constantly in mind, I must point out that I am a linguist and that I have approached his work chiefly through his language. The language of a writer, I believe, is the key to his work: its analysis provides the best approximation of his meaning. I have, however, not allowed myself the luxury of detailed stylistic analysis.

Rajendra Singh

Université de Montréal

Acknowledgments

I am indebted to Giri Raj Singh for sharing my initial enthusiasm for the work of Prasad and for explaining some of the intricacies of *Kamayani* during my formative years, to Professor Sylvia Bowman for inviting me to write the book for Twayne, and to Professor Mohan Lal Sharma for persuading her to invite me to do it.

The actual writing of the book was made possible by a Senior Research Fellowship from the Shastri Indo-Canadian Foundation. I am grateful to the foundation and to its staff, particularly Mrs. Kay De La Ronde, Mr. Robert Stevenson, and Mr. Prem Mallik. During my tenure as a Senior Research Fellow in India, I was attached to Banaras Hindu University. I am thankful to Mr. Om Prakash Govil, registrar of that university, for taking care of my day-to-day needs and to Dr. Vijaipal Singh, head of the University's Hindi Department, for not only talking to me about Prasad but also for introducing me to the poet's son, Mr. Ratna Shankar.

Since most of Prasad's works have not been translated into English, I have had to supply my own translations. My burden was, however, considerably lightened by Mr. Jaikishan Das Sadani, who readily gave permission for use of his translation of *Kamayani*. Without his cooperation it would have taken me perhaps another decade to complete this book.

Finally, I am thankful to Mrs. Pierette Parent for typing the preliminary draft of an unreadable manuscript full of exotic names. The penultimate draft was typed by an old and dear friend, Vibhuti Sharma, "for the love of Hindi literature." I am deeply indebted to him. The final draft was typed by Mrs. Sharon Coppa. I am indebted to her for doing an excellent job.

Chronology

1889 Jaishankar Prasad born in Banaras, son of Devi Prasad.
1891 Death of father.
1900 Travels to places of Hindu pilgrimage with mother.
1904 Death of mother.
1906 Death of elder brother. Assumes the responsibility of family business.
1909 *Urvashi*, a closet drama.
1910 *Expression of Sorrow* [*Shokochvas*], an elegy on the death of Edward VII.
1912 *Shadow* [*Chhaya*], a collection of short stories. *Flowers of the Garden* [*Kanan Kusum*], a collection of lyrics.
1914 *The Pilgrim of Love* [*Prem-Pathik*], a narrative in verse.
1915 *Rajyashri*, a play.
1918 *Chitradhar*, a collection of poems. *The Waterfall* [*Jharna*], a collection of lyrics.
1921 *Vishakha*, a play.
1922 *Ajatshatru*, a play.
1925 *Tears* [*Ansoo*], a lyrical narrative.
1926 *The Nag Campaign of Janmejay* [*Janmejay ka Nagyagya*], a play. *Echo* [*Pratidhwani*], a collection of short stories.
1927 *Rajyashri*, revised edition. *Kamana*, an allegorical play.
1928 *The House of Pity* [*Karunalay*], a play in verse. *The Importance of Maharana* [*Maharana ka Mahatva*], a narrative in verse. *Skandgupta*, a play.
1929 *The Lighthouse* [*Akash Deep*], a collection of short stories. *The Skeleton* [*Kankal*], a novel. *One Sip* [*Ek*

Ghunt], a one-act play. *The Storm* [*Andhi*], a collection of short stories.
1931 *Chandragupta*, a play.
1933 *Tears*, revised edition. *Dhruwaswamini*, a play. *The Wave* [*Lahar*], a collection of lyrics.
1935 *Kamayani*, an epic.
1936 *The Web* [*Indrajal*], a collection of short stories.
1937 Dies of consumption, November 15. *Poetry and Art and Other Essays* [*Kavya aur Kala Tatha anya Nibandh*], a collection of critical essays published posthumously. *Iravati*, a posthumously published incomplete novel.
1956 *The Music of Prasad* [*Prasad Sangit*], a collection of songs published posthumously.

Chapter One

The Man, the Place, and the Times

Early Hindi Literature: From Chivalry to Decadence

Although the history of Hindi literature is as long and as complex as the history of any European literature, its broad outlines, fortunately, can be sketched out within the limited space of a few pages without doing too much violence to its richness and complexity. Written in dialects other than Khari Boli,[1] the dialect which later became Standard Hindi, early Hindi literature was characterized "mainly by poetry of three kinds, each predominating in a different period of time."[2] The first period, commonly known as the Heroic Age, was a period of court poetry and lasted from about the middle of the eighth century until about the end of the fourteenth. The next two centuries saw the birth and development of *Bhakti* ("devotional") poetry. The period preceding the Modern Age was characterized by another type of court poetry, encouraged and patronized by the Moghul courts of pre-British India.

The earliest specimens of Hindi literature, some dating back to the eighth century, are poems composed by court bards for the benefit of their royal patrons. They deal with love, war, and chivalry, often with a generous mixture of undisguised flattery. The best example of this type of poetry is Chand Bardai's *The Saga of Prithvi Raj* [*Prithvi Raj Raso*], composed during the twelfth century. It is generally considered to be the first really important landmark of Hindi poetry or, for that matter, of Hindi literature as nonpoetic literature is a relatively recent development in Hindi. The main ingredient of the poetry of this period is, as exemplified in the following lines from Bardai, *vir* ("heroic") *rasa* ("predominant mood"):[3]

> They thrust with sword-edge biting
> They shout the shout of smiting
> They crouch from weapons sweeping
> They watch the steel blade leaping.[4]

The Heroic Age was characterized by continual warfare among the petty, rival Hindu kingdoms of North India. While these rivalries produced some very good heroic poetry, they made North India a particularly easy target of Muslim invasion. "By the end of the fourteenth century," observes Friend, "Muslim power over North India was consolidated and complete. The results of war, invasion, and then subjection to a foreign ruler with an alien culture turned people's thoughts and emotions inward, and they looked to God for solace and inspiration."[5] The resultant inner quest characterizes the Hindi literature of the next two centuries. It produced the great Hindi poets Kabir (c. 1440–1518), Surdas (c. 1478–1585), and Tulsidas (c. 1532–1623). It is commonly regarded as the golden age of Hindi literature.

Kabir attacked the meaningless rituals of Hinduism and Islam and in his search for a simple, honest morality went as far as to claim that

> The Puranas[6] and Korans are empty words:
> I have raised up the curtain
> And seen (them [for] what they are)
> Kabira utters these words from experience,
> And he knows
> All others are untrue.[7]

He "promoted the blending of Hindu and Muslim cultures by stressing the one-ness of God and His love for humanity."[8] He had

The Man, the Place, and the Times

no patience with a religion that allowed killing and encouraged discrimination and meaningless sacrifice:

> Who taught the widow to rush into the flames
> Of the funeral pyre of her beloved?
> Who to Love this mystery revealed
> To find in sacrifice full consumation?[9]

He delighted in paradox and in juxtaposing opposite images, and his poetry is often very complex in spite of its superficial simplicity:

> He is musician as well as the dancer;
> The eye and the dance, the ear and the sound.
>
> Closed are the gates to this scent-laden garden,
> The flowers they hide, without sight we perceive,
> As the wise may perceive my song's hidden meaning.[10]

Tulsidas, whose moral teachings define popular Hinduism in North India, wrote of the sacrifices and victories of the Aryan hero Ram. His religious lyrics define the very spirit of the Bhakti Movement: Too oft from Thee I turned my gaze/Towards a world of sparkling toys;/But turn not Thou Thy countenance from me."[11]

His best-known book, the book North India lives by, is *The Lake of Ram's Life and Deeds* [*Ramcharita Manas*], more popularly known as simply the *Ramayana*. Referring to it, Ainslie Embree says: "Westerners used to say that Tulsidas' work was the Bible of India, but that comparison is inadequate now, for Tulsidas' book is probably better known in North India than the Bible in any country in the West."[12] It is interesting to note that Atkins's translation of *Ramcharita Manas* contains a sixteen-page appendix in which he lists lines and couplets from it that have acquired proverbial status in the Hindi-speaking world. These proverbial lines and couplets, a random selection of which is given below, underline the moral tone of the book:

> That's not strange! Many people are fine in their talk,
> Yet but few of them by their own counsel will walk.[13]
>
> These four are as one—
> Daughter, sister, and wife of a brother or son.[14]
>
> Not a one but was struck by the serpent of care;
> Not a one but dark error found in him its lair.[15]
>
> Those greedily sensu'l and unsatisfied,
> Like crows, are of all other people afraid.[16]

Regarded by many Hindi speakers as the biography of God, *Ramcharita Manas* portrays the life and adventures of Ram. The framework of a hero's life provides the poet the opportunity to examine and express the entire gamut of human relations and emotions. He can effectively describe the subtle diplomacy of a first encounter:

> Then Sita with modesty looked up again,
> And saw just before her the young princely twain.
> As on handsome Ram she turned a full look,
> The thought of her father's vow scarce could she brook.[17]
> Her maids, when they saw her now under the sway
> Of the prince, said, "Let's go, we fear to delay."
> With a smile and a hint that the others could borrow,
> Said one, "We'll come here at the same time tomorrow."[18]

as well as the wrath of an enraged Brahman:

> You think me a Brahman and give me that name;
> I'll show you the Brahmanhood I wish to claim!
> My bow is the ladle; my shaft the oblation;
> My anger the flame of a fierce conflagration;
> Great well-equipt armies the sacrifice fuel;
> The animals offered are kings slain in duel;[19]

The overall tone of the epic, however, is unquestionably moral. It is a mirror not only for kings and princes but also for ordinary men and women. A compendium of homely truths and moral precepts, it is the work of a dedicated follower. Poetry and religion live side by side in it and its morality and poetry seem to inspire each other. In the hands of a lesser poet, it could have easily degenerated into a catalogue of precepts to live by, but Tulsidas gives real meaning to the notion of "moral imagination."

Self-denial and sublimation were the keynotes of Bhakti literature, and it emphasized sacrifice, religiousity, and a heaven in which the universe unfolds the way it should. It almost insisted on a nonhuman interpretation of expressions of purely human desires and fantasies.[20] It did, however, achieve great poetic heights.

By the seventeenth century, a new type of court poetry, patronized by the Moghul courts, came into existence. Secular in character, it "adopted the rules of Sanskrit poetics and imitated and elaborated on old forms."[21] It is sensuous, erudite, and technically perfect, but lacks vigor and inspiration, perhaps a just reflection of the declining political and moral life of Hindi-speaking India. Very often, the poets of this period, generally known as the *Riti* Period, substitute technical virtuosity for art and wordplay for poetry. One of the best-known poets of this age is Bihari (c. 1603–1663), whose *Satsai*, a collection of seven hundred couplets, is perhaps the most representative work of the era. It certainly contains some of its best poetry.

The rather dramatic end of the Moghul Empire and the full-fledged arrival of the West on the Indian scene introduced some new elements that have shaped the development of Hindi literature since the middle of the nineteenth century. Referring to some of these elements, Friend observes: "During the nineteenth century, communications by road, railway, and postal and telegraph service were improved. The printing press stimulated journalism and book production. Christian missionaries were helping to develop literature in regional languages and were exercising a socially democratizing influence as well. Universities were established teaching Western literature, thereby stimulating the development of the short-story, novel and essay. The teaching of Western philosophy gave rise to the concepts of nationalism and social reform."[22] The introduction of these elements ushered Hindi literature into the Modern Age.

Modern Hindi Literature: The Beginnings

The initial stage of the Modern Age in Hindi literature is commonly referred to as the Bhartendu Period (roughly about 1860–1900). It was characterized by vigorous literary activity and led to a great awakening which gave Hindi literature the various dimensions it needed to develop into a truly modern literature. During this period, Hindi prose literature made substantial strides. Novels began to be written and good journalism flourished. Drama also got something of a substantial start through the plays of Bhartendu Harishchandra (1850–1885).

Its main achievement was the establishment of Khari Boli as the chief literary dialect. The importance of this observation should be obvious from the following statement by Vatsyayan: "In a contemporary context, Hindi literature means exclusively the literature written in the Khari Boli, the language of the Delhi-Meerut region. Yet, as a generally accepted literary medium maintaining a uniform standard and continuity, Khari Boli is barely a century old, and as the channel of the main stream of poetry it was established only with the beginning of the present century."[23] "The acceptance of Khari Boli as the normal medium for Hindi verse," according to McGregor, "signalized a definitive parting from the older literary traditions of North India."[24]

The credit for the triumph of Khari Boli as the chief literary medium of Hindi is usually given to Pandit Mahavir Prasad Dwivedi (1868–1938), who, as editor of the influential journal *Sarasvati*, "devoted himself energetically to the reform and propagation" of Khari Boli.[25]

Dwivedi's influence, however, did not do much for the creative spirit. Most of the poets who published in *Sarasvati* during his editorship, command only historical interest and their poetry is "savorless, preachy, matter of fact and coarse."[26]

Though it was a period of enormous activity and prolific writers, its literary output is, at best, mediocre. The poetry, as noted already, is heavy and didactic, its drama theatrical and melodramatic, and its prose polemical. Although modern Hindi literature as we know it would not have been possible without the pioneering efforts of the writers of this period, it was essentially a period of promise rather than literary achievement. The promise was fulfilled only in the next generation.

Modern Hindi Literature: Chhayavad

"It is only with the end of the First World War," Vatsyayan correctly points out, "that we really enter the Modern age: as for contemporary trends a discussion might quite reasonably start from a generation later. Elsewhere critics have talked of an age of confusion and an age of anxiety: in Hindi the two were contemporaneous and almost synonymous."[27]

Chhayavad, a romantic movement against religious and didactic writers like Dwivedi and Harishchandra, can be said to have inaugurated the Modern Age in Hindi. In a tradition where the age had always been more important than the individual, Chhayavad sought to establish the expression of individual sensibility as the new goal. The new poetic movement was "an aesthetic subjective movement, a personal revolt against formalism and didacticism. Like the Bhakti movement of six centuries earlier, it was a cry of the heart against the straitjacket of tradition. The poet had found that there was something which was his very own and that he wanted more than anything else to say it; he chafed against the inadequacy of the instruments handed down to him—the language, the verse forms, the meters, the techniques and the taboos—and by the very intensity of need built new ones."[28]

Among those who reacted positively to "the new sensibility," Jaishankar Prasad stands preeminent. He is generally regarded as the first and foremost practitioner of Chhayavad. His whole literary output, as we shall see, is marked with features normally associated with romanticism. His work is consistently concerned with an expression of "the new sensibility." Although other writers have sometimes been credited with having inaugurated Chhayavad, a serious chronological study of early Chhayavad publications clearly indicates that it is Prasad who should be given that credit. Sushama Pal correctly observes: "While some scholars regard Prasad as the inaugurator of Chhayavad others think the title belongs to Pant. Nand Dulare Bajpai credits Pant for having inaugurated the movement on the basis of his *Uchhavas* which was published in 1920. But the fact is that Prasad came before Pant. By 1919, he had already published *Jharana*. It contains his compositions from the period 1909–1917. . . . These poems constitute the first authentic expression of the essential elements of Chhayavad. It is, therefore, Prasad who must be given the credit."[29]

The other major figures of Chhayavad were Sumitranandan Pant (1900–1977), Nirala (1896–1961), and Mahadevi Varma (born 1907). Prasad inaugurated the movement with the publication of *The Waterfall* [*Jharana*] in 1918. It was soon followed by Nirala's *Anonymous* [*Anamika*], the first version of which was published in 1922; Pant's *Leaves* [*Pallav*], published in 1928; and Varma's *Frost* [*Nihar*], published in 1930. These publications established Chhayavad as the style of the day.

Chhayavad is characterized by (1) subjectivism, (2) an element of mysticism, (3) love of Nature, (4) a spirit of boldness and rebellion, and (5) a concern for a new language that emphasized concreteness, sensuousness, and musicality. Although all these elements are present in all Chhayavadi writers, Nature found her highpriest in Pant, mysticism its chief voice in Verma, and the spirit of rebellion its most vocal and articulate spokesman in Nirala.

Refusing to have anything to do with a God that "neither talks nor hears,"[30] the Chhayavadi poet wanted to seek a new world and forge a revolution:

The Man, the Place, and the Times

> Joy of the year, friend Syama,
> Wash us and swell us with your joy;
> Drive, as a current a straw,
> Myself before you, and open the way
> Into your world of tumult and awe!
> > Arouse us, great cloud,
> > Impel us ahead;
> > Teach us, O my bold
> > Friend Syama, the way of revolt![31]

even if the price to be paid was personal pain and alienation:

> Back from the empty horizon
> Why does my echo come back
> Broken, sad, and almost lost,
> Miserable like an insane woman?[32]

Sorrow is, in fact, a major ingredient of Chhayavad. Mahadevi Varma's account of its role in her poetry can be legitimately read as Chhayavad's defense of sorrow: "Sorrow, the poetry of my private life, is capable of uniting the universe. Our unlimited pleasures may not be enough to take us to the first step of the ladder of humanity, but we can't shed a single tear without sharing in that humanity. Man wants to enjoy happiness all by himself, but he wants to share his sorrow."[33]

Although Chhayavad owes much to influences from outside Hindi, it must not be forgotten that the Chhayavadi poet drew considerably from Indian philosophy and the native Bhakti tradition. Mahadevi Varma, a major Chhayavad figure, herself has observed: "The quest for the mysterious, a rational principle of our literature of knowledge, became, albeit with the help of our sufi and saint poets, an integral part of our emotional existence. It expressed itself in such an artistic way that it satisfied both the heart and the mind. Our river of mystery flowed between Kabir's hatha yoga and metaphysical paradoxes and Jayasi's delicate descriptions of love and tenderness. It may be too early to say exactly what we have given to the Modern Age."[34]

The Sociopolitical Context

The two great movements of Prasad's time were "the challenge to outmoded values in Indian society and the growth of national aspirations for freedom."[35] Both were reactions to the impact of Western culture. The teachings of Western philosophy and literature gave rise to nationalism, which, in turn, activated a renewed interest in Indian culture and a desire for political freedom. Gandhi (1869–1948), with his strategy of passive resistance, became the chief spokesman for India's new political aspirations. The renewed interest in India's past was given the shape of a reform movement by Swami Dayanand Saraswati (1824–1883).

Gandhi's political and moral philosophy and achievements are too well known to warrant any discussion here. The main thrust of Saraswati's teachings was that popular Hinduism had mistakenly incorporated various things for which ancient religious texts of Hinduism gave no authority. The main task facing Hindus, he argued, was to purify Hinduism by discarding the illegitimate conventions and rituals, such as idol worship and untouchability, that had crept into it over the centuries. A purified Hinduism, he believed, would take India to a future no less glorious than its past.

Although Prasad's work does not contain any direct references to Saraswati's teachings, he must have been familiar with them for they were very much in the air. Both of them were, at any rate, concerned with redefining Hindusim by looking more closely at its traditional sources. While Saraswati wrote reformist tracts, Prasad went about the task of reinterpreting Hinduism in quieter and more literary terms. Both of them, however, believed Hinduism was not really what it was generally supposed to be.

No discussion of the first few decades of the twentieth century can be considered complete without a mention of Prem Chand (1880–1936).[36] Though he is generally regarded as Hindi's best novelist, his abiding social concerns made him a social force as well. His realistic fiction portrayed the harsh realities of peasant life in North India. It is one of the paradoxes of life in India that the emergence of the introspective and romantic school of Chhayavad "coincides with the political and social ferment of the twenties and thirties, the age portrayed so harshly and painfully in the mature novels of Prem Chand."[37] Whereas the Chhayavadi poets chose to create an imaginary landscape, Prem Chand decided to cope with the world around him, unpleasant and harsh as it was. But perhaps the paradox is only an apparent one. The harsh realism of Prem Chand and the romanticism of Chhayavadi writers represent the two sides of the oppression of the individual: whereas the voice of Prem Chand was the voice of the social being whose sense of justice was enraged, the voice of Chhayavad was the voice of the individual who needed more than anything else, to express himself.

The Man

Born in the holy city of Banaras in 1889, Prasad, one of Hindi's greatest writers, was the son of a relatively wealthy tobacco merchant. The family enjoyed tremendous prestige, comparable in certain ways to that of the local royal family.[38] His grandfather was a generous patron of the arts and regularly entertained poets, artists, and musicians. As a child he traveled a bit with his parents and had a fairly smooth "establishment" life.

His father, unfortunately, died in 1901, leaving the family's business in the hands of his elder brother, apparently not the best possible manager. The business suffered serious losses. The difficulties were compounded when his mother and elder brother also died, forcing him to assume total responsibility for the entire operation at a relatively young age. He accepted, perhaps somewhat reluctantly, the responsibility, and worked reasonably hard to restore the family's lost fortune and prestige.

As children are taken for granted in most joint families, not too much information is available about his early childhood. Apparently, he lived, as most middle-class and upper-middle-class

Indian children do, a nondescript life, a life controlled by parents and seniors. His father's economic independence, however, allowed him the luxury of a private tutor.

Although his formal education was somewhat restricted—he never attended a secondary school—he was fortunate enough in having a tutor who taught him Sanskrit, Persian, and English at home. The lack of formal education did not, fortunately, deprive him of the opportunity to read the classics not only of Hindi and Sanskrit literature but also of English and Greek literature. His tutor was a poet, though a minor one, and helped him develop his poetic talents. Prasad respected his tutor and often consulted him later in life.

His adolescent years seem to have been quite normal. Although most Hindi critics believe his life after childhood to have been full of crises of one sort or another, and within the context of the joint family it probably was, he seems to have led a rather uneventful life. There are no indications of personal revolt, but they are, it must be pointed out, rather rare in the Indian context. He managed to combine life, literature, and business with a minimum of personal discomfort.

He died of consumption in 1937. Although he did not live to be fifty, he left behind him an enormous body of literature, even a portion of which would have assured him of a prestigious place not only in the annals of Hindi literature but Indian literature in general. His total output of some thirty books, which include lyrics and literary criticism, plays and poems, novels and an epic, unquestionably makes him what native tradition recognizes him to be: a *Maha Kavi* ("a great poet").

A man of medium height, Prasad, according to a friend, had "a fair complexion, a broad forehead, and a round face."[39] He was a vegetarian and a total abstainer. He loved flowers and had a small garden of his own.

A true devotee of Shiva, he worked hard, dividing his time among writing, worship, business, and physical fitness. He kept mostly to himself and shunned publicity. He did not participate in *kavi-sammelans* ("poetic gatherings") and even when he could not avoid attending them he refrained from reciting his own work.[40] He did so only once and even then he had to be ordered to perform by his guru. Although his doubts and conflicts find articulate expression in his work, in private life he maintained the "calm of mind, passions all spent" posture. He had none of the nervousness and rebellion normally associated with young romantic writers.

Total acceptance of the rich complexities of life, in fact, seems to have been his guiding principle. Business to him was apparently no more abhorrent than death: both were integral parts of life. Commenting on this aspect of his personality, Bajpai observes: "I always saw this Banarasi colour in Prasad. Some people were fascinated by his cheerful disposition and some by his sociability. No man, however, saw the real man behind all this, a man who enjoyed his own work, desired no fame, and remained untouched by both praise and criticism."[41]

He was, according to Sahney, a perfect gentleman, who never said a harsh word even about his worst opponents and "maintained his noble silence even when his opponent railed at his loudest."[42] When critics attacked him fiercely in the columns of *Sudha*, characterizing his masterpieces *Chandragupta* and *Skandgupta* as elaborate tissues of falsehoods and trickery, he kept silent. Years later, when "those very men who had attacked him came to see him he received them with such warmth of affection that they were thoroughly disillusioned and acknowledged the greatness of the man they had unwittingly maligned."[43] If any man was ever a hero to his valet it was, Sahney says, Prasad.[44]

His "noble silence" finds poetic expression in the frankly autobiographical lyric entitled "Autobiography" ["Atma Katha"]:

> How can I tell big tales of this small life today
> Isn't it better to listen to others and be quiet
> What will you do with the innocent story anyway?
> Moreover, it isn't time yet.[45]

He was a voracious reader. He knew Sanskrit and Hindi literature like the palm of his hand. He was also well read in Persian, Urdu, Bengali, and English. It is generally believed that he had a mere bowing acquaintance with English literature, but Sahney contends that his knowledge of English literature was at once extensive and profound and that he was particularly fond of Spenser, Shakespeare, Milton, Wordsworth, Shelley, Arnold, and Rossetti.[46]

He also read Greek philosophy, history, and literature in translation and was fond of Homer, Sophocles, Plato, Aristotle, and Thucydides. Of the great Italians, he loved Dante in particular and had read *The Divine Comedy* in Carey's translation.[47]

His relationship to literature and knowledge is summed up beautifully by Sahney: "His devotion to literature was infinite, his curiosity inexhaustible, and his memory infallible. I have not known a more voracious reader than Prasad; and yet he was a man of invincible originality."[48]

Prasad was very fond of classical Indian music. "Nothing moved him like an old melody."[49] In order to listen to good music, he would go to the house of Sideshwari Bai, a well-known courtesan of Banaras. *Samrasa*, or harmony, was the guiding principle of his life, and music to him was harmonization par excellence.

He worked steadily, and not spasmodically. He would get up, take a walk, do some exercises, and write a few pages. After shopping hours, he would come home and write some more, "often into the later hours."[50] The regularity and certainty with which he went about conducting himself were indicative of a man totally at peace with himself.

The Place

A stay-at-home type, Prasad went out of Banaras only three or four times. Banaras, a teeming city of religious profundities and moral profanities, remained the locus of his existence throughout life, and Banaras was an interesting place to be in. Here is Madan Gopal's description of the city around 1850:

The Man, the Place, and the Times

Being the principal pilgrimage center of the Hindus, it attracted from all parts of India not only devout pilgrims in search of salvation but also merchants looking for customers, and charlatans, cheats and quacks looking for victims; also all types of hangers-on and parasites, deprived of the patronage of the courts of the Moghuls in Delhi and of the Nawabs of Oudh, Lucknow flocked to Banaras of those days. The city also provided succour to talented artists on the one hand, and to pandits renowned for their scholarship and priestly traditions on the other. Not only the Maharaja of Banaras—a great patron of arts in his own right—but also some of the wealthy aristocratic families of the city extended patronage to all artists, be they poets or musicians, dancers or prostitutes.[51]

Banaras, or Varanasi as it is traditionally known, is a colorful, though somewhat muddled, city, situated about 350 miles southeast of Delhi. Its non-Anglicized name is a compound noun made up of *Varuna* (a tributary of the Ganges) and *Assi* (literally "eighty" but referring to the eightieth bathing station, or *ghat*, situated where the Varuna empties into the Ganges). From Mani Kani Ka, where the Hindus cremate their dead, to Assi, the western bank of the Ganges provides a dramatic introduction to Hinduism. Beggars and religious priests compete for the attention of the newly arrived pilgrim as the religious music and chanting in the numerous temples in the background continue against shouts of "Har, har Mahadev."[52]

A half-hour stay at one of these bathing stations can provide some serious lessons in the basic structure of Hindu society just as reading the Sears Catalogue can provide an illuminating introduction to the sociology of middle-class America. The priestly recitation of religious verses is interrupted only by an ugly outburst of foul language to force the untouchable or the beggar to leave and the moral concentration of the worshiper is broken only by the sight of a beautiful female body unable to hide itself in the wet sari.[53] Chance encounters defy laws of probability and diamond-studded golden bracelets push broken brass-plates of the beggar as the family priest recounts the results of his latest espionage mission undertaken for the benefit of his client. There is a story here every step of the way. The lonely recluse, the promiscuous businessman, the seductive widow, the serious scholar, and the sadistic beggar-lord jostle with one another in blissful anonymity.

Banaras at the time of Prasad was also a center of Hindi literature. It was here that Bhartendu Harishchandra launched his *Poet's Voice* [*Kavi Vachan Sudha*], the first Hindi monthly, in 1867 and *Harishchandra Magazine*, a journal devoted to the propagation of the spoken language of the common people, in 1873. Banaras was also the home of Modern Hindi's first great novelist Prem Chand and of the Nagari Pracharini Sabha, a society devoted to spreading Hindi language and literature. It was also the seat of the Banaras Hindu University, a major institution dedicated to the study of both Hindu and secular knowledge. From literary and academic points of view, it was a lively place for a Hindi writer to grow up.

But above all Banaras was a city of the followers of Shiva, the Indian god of energy and infinite patience. Legend has it that when nobody wanted the poison recovered from the ocean, he drank it, earning the epithet *nil-kanth* ("blue throat"), to stop a fight between the gods and the demons. The multiplicity of Banaras has a focus: Shiva. Prasad was a devout follower of Shiva. Bajpai calls him the Modern Shaiva.[54]

A part of the greater Banaras that he liked very much and went to often with his friends for picnics was Sarnath, where the Buddha reputedly preached his first sermons. Sarnath is a quiet retreat of majestic Buddhist shrines and carefully preserved ruins of Buddhist monasteries. Whereas the temple and ghat dominated heart of Banaras is full of noise and ritual, Sarnath provides an impressively quiet landscape in which to sort out the noises. Sarnath is enough to make one fall in love with Buddhism. Buddhism does, in fact, dominate many of his works. The Buddhist message of *Shanti*—peace that passes understanding—can still be heard in Sarnath, and equally clearly in the works of Prasad.

Chapter Two

The Early Years

Juvenilia and Experiments

Though language is automatic, style is a matter of choice. Learning to make choices one feels comfortable with takes time. Prasad took about a decade to learn to write his way. It is a decade of influences, shadows of literary giants and ghosts, and of considerable, though intrinsically poor, literary output. It is, however, amazing in its variety: lyric, narrative, short story, closet drama, and essay. Some of the output of this period is simply bad, and of only historical interest. Prasad seems to be trying everything, following a lead here, an idol there. But one must begin and learn to fall.

The earliest work, a few poems in Braj, a couple of plays, and a few prose pieces in Khari Boli, is only of historical interest[1]. The subjects are mostly traditional, and the language generally rather deadening. There are, however, occasional indications of a new voice, as in this very human and individualistic complaint against an invisible God: "What shall I do with a God/That neither talks, nor hears, nor helps."[2]

The experimentation with Braj, however, ended soon. Prasad, under the influence of Dwivedi, started writing in Khari Boli. The experiments in Khari Boli, collected in *Flowers of the Garden* [*Kanan Kusum*], were first published in 1913. Although *Flowers of the Garden* is mostly an experiment, there are rather strong indications of a new idiom in it.

In *Flowers of the Garden*, Prasad not only brings the didactic kind of poetry advocated by Dwivedi to perfection but also breaks new ground by introducing free verse. The poems in free verse, such as "India" ["Bharat"], "Brave Child" ["Vir Balak"], "Anniversary of Shri Krishna" ["Shri Krisna Jayanti"] and "Sculptural Beauty" ["Shilpa-Saundarya"], are not very impressive. Some of them are, however, bold experiments that indicate a new voice in clear terms.

The preference for Khari Boli is announced in unmistakable terms in the revised edition of *The Pilgrim of Love* [*Prem Pathika*], a poem published earlier in Braj in 1906. In 1914, Prasad revised the poem and rewrote it in Khari Boli. The author's preface to the revised edition reads:

A small book like this does not need a big preface. It should be enough to point out that I wrote it in Braj some eight years ago and that a part of it was published in the first volume of *Indu*.[3] This is its rewritten, revised, free-verse version in Hindi.[4]

The use of "Hindi" in the preface is suggestive of the definitional change Prasad helped bring about.

The poem, like its earlier Braj counterpart, describes the tragic separation of two young lovers in their own words. When they accidentally meet one another after years of painful separation, Kishor tells his story to a stranger in a strange village, but the stranger turns out to be his childhood beloved, Chameli. They listen to each other till dawn "Started making its golden world" and vow to leave "for the land of peace."[5]

Prasad was an idealist and *The Pilgrim of Love* is "the rapturous pean or song of ideal love" which "emphasizes the fact that friends are extremely rare and that those who pass for friends are often mere base flatterers in the guise of friends."[6]

Although it is, like the older version, melodramatic and sentimental, it shows greater control. The language of the newer version is far more polished and some of its metaphors rise quite beyond the hackneyed comparisons of the Braj version. There is even an effort to bring in some reality-based irony, as when

The Early Years

Chameli tells Kishor to "consider it only a story."[7] The broken heart has since time immemorial been compared with a crushed flower, but Prasad brings in a new dimension: "Who can hear the breaking of the flower of heart?"[8] And the golden dawn has never been described as the moment when: "The yellow heat started making its golden world."[9]

The revised version leaves much to be desired, but the revisions indicate that a new voice is just around the corner—as a matter of fact, just four years away. The subtle originality and stylistic sophistication exhibited in the revised edition of *The Pilgrim of Love* lead directly to what is distinctively Prasadian in *The Waterfall* [*Jharana*], first published in 1918.

His first dramatic effort, *Gentleman* [*Sajjan*], published in 1912, is a rather disappointing traditional play that attempts to contrast the generosity of Yudhishther with the ungrateful nature of Duryodhan.[10] It follows all the principles of Sanskrit dramaturgy but has very little to recommend itself. Equally immature and disappointing is *Penance* [*Prayshchit*], first published in 1913. Apparently inspired by Shakespeare's *Macbeth*, Prasad attempts to portray the downfall of Jay Chand, the Benedict Arnold of Indian History. Both *Gentleman* and *Penance* are, however, only experiments, though the former has been called "the first original tragedy in Hindi."[11] They do not, it must be pointed out, compare unfavorably with other plays, such as those of Bhartendu Harishchandra, of the period. They seem disappointing mainly because one expects a bit more from Prasad.

The outline of a new dramatic aesthetic can, however, be seen developing in *Rajyashri* (1915), a play dealing with the reign of Harshavardhan.[12] It marks a turning point not only in the dramatic career of Prasad but also in the history of Hindi drama. A short play of only thirty-nine pages, the first edition of *Rajyashri* is a brave effort to move away from the claptrap of traditional dramaturgy. The play is dominated by the character of Rajyashri, Harsha's sister. Strong and beautiful, she fights her way through a seemingly endless chain of intrigues and plots of lust and greed.

Although *Rajyashri* has its shortcomings—at times it is dull and pseudopoetic—the essential elements of Prasaian drama—insightful characterization, conflict, historical imagination, and intensity—are all present in it. As the playwright matures, the shortcomings disappear to give such materpieces as *Chandragupta, Skandgupta,* and *Dhruwaswamini*. *Rajyashri*, Prasad's first historical play, marks the beginning of a new type of drama in Hindi. In spite of its shortcomings, *Rajyashri* makes other contemporary plays appear melodramatic and immature. In unmistakable terms, it announces the coming of age of Hindi literary drama.

The medium of the short story is also explored, and the result, *Shadow* [*Chhaya*], was published in 1912. It is also a mixed blessing: promising, but disappointing in itself. Its original (1912) edition contained five short stories, including "Village" ["Gram"], Prasad's first attempt at short fiction, and "Tansen," Prasad's first historical short story. *Shadow*, according to Gupta, is "Hindi's first original collection of short-stories."[13] Their claim to importance is, however, only historical.

Even "The Moon" ["Chanda"], the best of the lot according to Gupta, is more of a miracle than a short story.[14] It is the story of a young girl who lets the man to whom she was once engaged be killed by a tiger because he refused to save her lover when the latter was struggling for life from the paws of a tropical beast. She takes her revenge but has nothing left to live for, and, therefore, kills herself, too. That two people should die an identical death seems a bit too theatrical, and the revenge melodrama is somewhat restricted in its appeal.

"Tansen," the first historical story by Prasad, is much better. It describes how the singer Ramprasad became the legendary Tansen. The historical authenticity of the story is difficult, if not impossible, to verify but the conversion of a singer into a legend is skillfully narrated. Although the story is called "Tansen," we never hear of Tansen till the penultimate paragraph and are left wondering why it should be called what it is. A musical match is arranged between Ramprasad and one of the slaves of his host's

The Early Years 21

wife. When the match concludes the host and hostess are convinced of the victory of their respective protégés. The host concludes: "Ramprasad, from today you are 'Tansen.' And Sausan is yours. But you must marry her."[15]

The story is slight, but Prasad makes a genuine effort to reconstruct the Moghul India of Akbar.[16] The story shows Prasad's fascination with Indian history, a fascination that will grow with time and help him construct such masterpieces as *Chandragupta* (1931) and *Iravati* (1937).

In spite of their obvious shortcomings, the works of the juvenile period quite clearly indicate an intense individual struggling very hard to find the right medium and the right style within that medium. He tries everything, almost simultaneously. He is eager to find himself, and learns his lessons, as we shall see, extremely well.

The Arrival of a New Voice

The first clear indication of the arrival of a new literary voice is to be found in *The Waterfall*, a collection of twenty-five lyrics first published in 1918. The publisher's preface claims: "The style of poetry that has come to be called *Chhayavad* was inaugurated with this collection. From that point of view, it is a very important collection."[17] *The Waterfall*, according to Sahney, "symbolizes the emergence of vital beauty out of inert matter, that beauty whose function, as Prasad himself says in the title-piece, is to 'cool the fever of life.'"[18]

Cast into an essentially Sufi mode with mystic overtones, most of the lyrics are about love.[19] The language is, however, mostly simple, polished, and able to bear the burden of some heavy mystical philosophizing. The images are real and concrete, often masked by a tenderness peculiarly Prasadian. Here is his description of a lover's request to be let in:

> Laden with snow drops, each thread of my blanket is wet
> And the west wind blows with the weight of cold

> The tender and beautiful body of the night is getting wet
> Touch, the rays of the dawn, open my dear, open the door.[20]

While most of the lyrics can be interpreted at the human level, some clearly require a mystic interpretation but even here the possibility that it is the beloved that has been given a divine status rather than that God is being treated as a beloved remains strong, giving these lyrics a sensuous quality rarely attempted in Hindi before Prasad and equally rarely captured by his successors: "Not satisfied of looking at you/Every day, I give you a new shape."[21]

Although there is a considerable amount of didacticism and mysticism in the lyrics of *The Waterfall*, even some of the more blatantly philosophical pieces, like "Command" ["Adesh"] contain the individualistic twist that points to the mature philosophical preoccupations of later work:

> Why this prayer and penance?
> Whose worship is this:
> Afraid of your own sins,
> You humiliate yourself.[22]

Symbolic of a new turn in the author's career, *The Waterfall* is, according to Premshankar, "a laboratory of lyrics,"[23] and although all the experiments conducted in this laboratory are not equally successful, enough of them establish the paradigm the author is going to follow. Though somewhat uneven, the better pieces in *The Waterfall* unmistakably announce a new voice to be reckoned with.

Although the imagery of *The Waterfall* is mostly traditional, Prasad occasionally gives the traditional images a refreshing twist: "Upon receiving from spring the summons on yellow paper/Trees have shed their leaves after drying them out."[24]

One of the favorite devices of *The Waterfall* is the use of internal question-answer pairs that provide the lyrics with a dramatic quality and a sense of movement:

The Early Years

>   Don't disappear to destroy the festival of life
>   Where? Some lonely spot?—Where there's no crowd
>   Far? But how far?[25]

The imagined questions and counterquestions render them into little one-act plays, where the actors have to be imagined though they can be heard through the narrator. Although the dramatic monologue is not traditionally recognized as a separate category in Hindi, the lyrics of *The Waterfall* provide some of the best dramatic monologues of early modern Hindi literature.

The technique is carried over even into lyrics devoted to Nature. The short question and the subtle imagined answer provide some of these lyrics with a dramatic musicality truly rare in Hindi:

>   The nightingale in the tree calls:
>   You there, somewhere? Are you?
>   Come, wherever you are
>   Tu-whit, Tu-where?
>   Thirsty, dying of thirst are the birds
>   Why do you want to become a killer?
>   Black gold, where're you?
>   Tu-Whit, Tu-Where?[26]

The moods covered in the lyrics of *The Waterfall* range from the utter despair of "Beloved" ["Priyatam"]—"This is your justice?/The pen trembles and the letter shakes"[27]—to the unshakable optimism of "Waiting for Spring" ["Vasant ki Pratiksa"]: "I keep cultivating my garden/For someday it is bound to blossom."[28] En route, one finds the uncertainty of "When" ["Kab"], the begging of "Request" ["Nivedan"], the dreaming of "Dreamland" ["Swapna-lok"], and the masochistic despondency of "To Neglect" ["Upeksa Karana"].

The lyrics of *The Waterfall* are, according to Sahney, "remarkable for their brevity, their passion, their imagination, their subjectivity, their mellifluousness, their picturesqueness, their flow of rhythm, their simplicity, their spontaneity, and their symbolism.

They are, indeed, perfect specimens of lyricism and have the rounded loveliness of dewdrops on lotus leaves."[29]

The year 1918 also saw the publication of an enlarged edition of *Shadow*. Prasad added six historical stories to the original five, only one of which was devoted, it would be recalled, to a historical figure, Tansen. The historical tales center around imaginary crucial moments in the lives of memorable figures such as Alexander and Ashoka.[30] "The Oath of Alexander" ["Sikandar Ki Shapatha"] shows Alexander as a less than honest man who does not hesitate to attack his Afghan enemy after dark and who orders the Indian soldiers helping his Afghan enemy slaughtered though he had promised them free passage. The story is intended as a patriotic tribute to the heroic deeds of these unsung heroes: "They lost their lives in an unknown place. Indians don't even know their names."[31]

Although the story smacks of sentimental parochialism, it is well constructed and succeeds in capturing the many lonely self-confrontations Alexander must have faced during his arduous voyage. And it does so in simple, effective language: "Alexander had been sitting there for quite some time. Darkness was spreading to hide the world as a cunning person attempts to hide his evil plans. Only an owl or two could be heard in the desolate battle-field."[32]

"Ashoka" shows the Buddhist emperor forced to resort to another demonstration of his power to bring peace.[33] Reluctantly, he orders his commander-in-chief to revive the terror that was once synonymous with his name: "There was a time in India when people used to tremble at the name of this very Ashoka. Why? Because he was a strict ruler. But when that Ashoka became known as a Buddhist, people assumed he was no longer capable of governing his empire. I want you to spread the terror of Ashoka once more."[34]

He also orders the Jains to be killed on sight. Ironically, his son gives refuge to some of his potential victims and his elder-brother, a Jain, is killed in compliance with his instructions. The outcome

The Early Years

of the desire to spread the terror of his name once again is a total ban on killing.

"The Liberation of Chittor" ["Chittor Uddhar"] deals with the life of a widowed daughter of the ruler of Chittor, who married her off to Hammir.[35] She considers herself unworthy of her husband, but he refuses to accept the doctrine according to which she should be blamed for the death of her first husband, and, when he turns out to be a real human being, she invites him to attack her father's kingdom when he happens to be away. Hammir does, and the widowed daughter becomes the legitimate queen of the little kingdom whose ruler had used her as a pawn in his political game.

The story is a powerful effort to describe the petty rivalries among various Indian rulers, the central concern of later plays like *Skandgupta* and *Chandragupta*, and the subtle psychological tensions in the mind of a delicate young girl taught to believe that widowhood is a sin for which the victim is responsible. The little princess of 'The Liberation of Chittor" foreshadows the powerful princess of *Dhruvaswamini* who refuses to be sacrificed by an impotent pillar of tradition.

"Jahanara" is the story of the declining years of Shahjahan, the Moghul emperor, who was dethroned and imprisoned by his son, Aurangzeb, and his daughter, Jahanara, who devotes her life to her dying father.[36] The story counterpoints Aurangzeb's relentless search for power against Jahanara's kindness and generosity. It ends on a rather sentimental note: a dying Jahanara and a repentant Aurangzeb.

Most of the stories of *Shadow* are somewhat sentimental, but that should not allow one to detract from their strength. They are simple and powerful narratives regarding totally or partially imaginary characters trying to cope with very real human problems: love, betrayal, faith, loyalty, and gratitude. The historical stories are remarkable not for their historical authenticity but for their humanization of historical characters that seem to have survived only as human legends. It is not important whether Alexander really broke the promise he gave the mistress of the Afghan fort or whether Aurangzeb really cried at his sister's death. What is important is that Alexander could have broken a promise and Aurangzeb could have cried.

The stories of *Shadow* move quickly. Their dialogue is sharp and free of verbiage. Here is the encounter between Ashoka and his imprisoned son, who has just been brought to the court:

> The King himself asked: "Your name?"
> Answer: "Kunal."
> Question: "Father's name?"
> Answer: "His Highness the Emperor Ashoka."
>
> . . . .
>
> Question: "Are you guilty of anything?"
> Answer: "I tried to stay away from any crime."
> Question: "Then, why have you been charged?"
> Answer: "Please ask your Chief Minister."[37]

The stories of *Shadow* establish Prasad's growing mastery of Khari Boli, the dialect chosen by him as his medium, his love of Indian history, and his fondness for lyrical intensity and dramatic tension. The stories added later show remarkable progress. The outlines of history provide the external framework which seems to provide the structural control missing in the rather loose romantic tales of the earlier edition.

The considerable progress made by Prasad can also be seen in his next dramatic effort, *Vishakha* (1921), an attempt to bring to life some unpublished chapters of ancient Indian history. It represents another step toward a distinctively Prasadian drama. The play revolves around the love affair between Vishakha and Chandralekha. Chandralekha is taken a prisoner by Buddhists to be released later by Nardeva, the King of Kashmir, who falls in love with her. Chandralekha's lack of interest in and rejection of Nardeva sets a complicated plot, involving espionage and impersonation by a Buddhist monk, the suicide of the queen, and half a dozen other intrigues and tragedies, into action. The play, however, ends on a conciliatory note: the king is forgiven and Chandralekha's father regains his land that had been given to the Buddha by the king's father. *Vishakha* depicts the decline of Buddha and gives a good indication of Prasad's concern with ancient Indian history. According to the preface, the story is constructed out of an incident from the first or second century B.C.

Ajatshatru (1922), a play regarding the conflict between Hinduism and Buddhism in ancient India,[38] and *Tears* [*Ansoo*], an intense and highly romantic long lyric, firmly establish the major characteristics of Prasadian drama and poetry.

A play about Buddhist India, *Ajatshatru* opens with the future King of Magadha[39] being told by a cousin to give up violence. His mother, however, does not approve of Buddha. She seeks his coronation, which is granted. Becoming king, however, only creates a series of problems for Ajatshatru, who, by the third act, ends up as a prisoner. He is released only through the intervention of those disciples of Buddha he had virtually imprisoned. The play ends on a happy note as all claims are settled and conflicts resolved, partly through the direct intervention of Buddha and partly through the acceptance of his doctrine of forgiveness by most of the parties involved.

Obviously concerned with the historical authenticity of the play, Prasad takes considerable pains to confirm the historicity of the major characters and events. He also makes a serious effort to reconstruct the social life of the period. Krishandas, in his introduction to the play, correctly observes: "So far, very little research has been conducted into the social life of our ancestors. But Prasad has utilized whatever information is now available."[40]

Impressed with the cyclic nature of history, Prasad attempts in *Ajatshatru* a dramatization of a chapter from an extremely critical period of ancient Indian history, a period characterized by a religious revolution of far-reaching consequences. The genesis of the revolution is described by Prasad himself in his preface to the play: "The masses were getting impatient with sacrificial Vedic rituals and with the authority of the pundits. This impatience led to the spread of Jainism and Buddhism. The spread of Jainism, non-violent in the extreme, was followed by Buddhism. It was a new compromise between the violent rituals of Vedism and the extremism of Jainism. Perhaps that is why Buddha designated his religion as *madhyama pratipada*. It was this religious revolution that forced the various nations of India to give up mutual destruction."[41]

Whereas *Vishakha* is a dramatization of the decline and fall of Buddhism, *Ajatshatru* is a dramatization of the petty intrigues and unjustifiable violence that led to the rise and spread of Buddhism, a religion built around not a clever theology and a sharp metaphysics but around human compassion and kindness and forgiveness.[42] Even our first encounter with Buddhism in the play brings the message home:

Bimbsar: "I am obliged, my lord, that you came."
Gautam: "King! No one obliges anyone. If there is anything in the world that can do anything, it is piety, which treats everyone equally."[43]

This dramatization of the rise of Buddhism inevitably leads Prasad to introduce a large number of petty intrigues to be counterpointed against the compelling simplicity of Buddha and his disciples: "Don't affectionate voice and behaviour control even wild animals?"[44] The power-hungry princes and their stooges are left disarmingly naked before the master-healer and his followers.

The motion generated by a relentless search for power is constantly challenged by the apparent passivity of Buddha. Movement and lack of movement, in fact, become the controlling images of the play:

Man wants a solid foundation, though he knows life is momentary. When the unknown messages written in bright stars disappear from

The Early Years 29

the blue sky, man gets busy with his *tandava*[45] of daily-struggle. Even then Nature tries to help him understand his mysterious fate by withdrawing the daylight. But he doesn't listen. He dies for fame and for power. He is not happy with his low but satisfying position. He has to climb, though he is bound to fall.[46]

Moving up and growing bigger are, according to our kings and princes, laws of nature. Here is a queen exhorting her son to realize his potential: "To grow bigger is the obvious law of nature. Why do you want to defy it? Prepare yourself to jump in the everlasting bright fire of ambition and destroy all those that oppose you."[47]

The everlasting bright fire of ambition, the queen forgets, is a fire nevertheless; and fire, according to another law of nature, burns and consumes.

The results of this pursuit of power and ambition leave Bajira, the princess, completely confused: "Man now considers warfare to be an art. Poets write about wars. They excite the barbarian's blood! Palaces have become prison-houses! Those who were once welcome guests are now prisoners."[48]

Buddha realizes the fragility of power so actively pursued by the petty princes and princesses around him. He refuses to be upset by the numerous scandals created to discredit him or to ask his disciples to punish all those bent upon destroying him: "You cannot hide the Sun-like Truth with a sieve. This everlasting movement will consume everyone. Why should I think of revenge?"[49]

The numerous feuds and intrigues are brought to an end when everyone, including Ajatshatru, realizes the irreparable psychological loss the pursuit of power can cause. The doctrine of forgiveness prevails and the young prince who in the beginning of the play was ready to beat up one of his professional hunters for not having brought him game has this to say toward the end of the play about the series of actions set in motion by him: "Forgive me, mother! War is frightening. So many women become helpless. The glory of warfare must be the figment of a sick imagination. It brings out the worst in man. The scene of the battlefield is truly frightening."[50]

When the play ends, the salutation "emperor," once considered the highest, is construed as an insult. The definitional change and the illocutionary force now attached to what used to be an expression of highest deference complete the circle:

Jivak: (Entering) "Emperor!"
Bimbsar: "Silent! If you don't know my name, call me a man. I don't want your insulting salutation."[51]

Ajatshatru is an ambitious play and though it establishes the Prasadian canon in unmistakable tones, it is not entirely without serious shortcomings. The plot is a bit too thick and the play occasionally suffers from a total lack of dramatic action. It is true that Prasad needs petty subplots in order to dramatize the serene quietude of Buddha, but one wonders if a whole host of them is needed. The play also abounds in purple passages that seem disproportionately long. It is true that a play concerned explicitly with two moralities is bound to have rhetorical expositions of the two points of view, but one wonders if the dramatist himself is not enjoying the rhetoric for its own sake. The change of hearts required to resolve the problem, though necessary to dramatically translate the message of forgiveness, also seems a bit forced. The major proponents of power and wealth seek and grant forgiveness toward the end of the play with almost an aggressive vulgarity. The change is not equally justified in each case. Some of the characters seem to accept it just because it is "in the air."

But, in spite of its weaknesses, *Ajatshatru* is a powerful play, the dramatic appeal of which transcends the socioculturally determined concerns of Buddhist India. Buddhism and Vedic Hinduism merely become names for the oppositions that mankind must learn to neutralize or to choose from. The choice, however, cannot be made once for all. It must be reexamined every so often.

The Early Years

Ajatshatru represents that aggregation of properties under which the rejection of ceaseless action becomes inevitable. In his other plays, the wheel stopped in *Ajatshatru* is reactivated.

Ajatshatru unquestionably establishes the new style of drama associated with Prasad. From now on, it is a matter of constant refinement only. *Ajatshatru* is a major play, not an experiment. The later plays represent improvements—in style and dramatic control—without deviating from the essentials established in *Ajatshatru*.

Ajatshatru was followed by *Tears*, a long romantic lyric of 252 lines first published in 1925. It is an expression of the "new sensibility" of Chhayavad in a forceful and personalized language that for many represents the hallmark of the new poetic style inaugurated by Prasad. It expresses the pain and the sorrow which is the inevitable lot of a romantic struggling to cope with a universe that has laws of its own, laws that do not conform to the romantic's blueprint. The Moving Finger moves on, and the romantic's inability to have even half a line canceled forces him to produce the 252 lines that constitute this long lyric to register his complaint, his pain and his deep sense of loss.

Sorrow and a deep sense of loss are, in fact, the pervading elements of *Tears*. The title page of the lyric offers the following paraphrase of the title:

>The condensed pain,
>Like a cloud of memory,
>Having turned into tears
>Is now going to rain.[52]

The poem begins with an open declaration of uncontrolable sorrow:

>Full of pain and misery
>Why does the heart play a sad song?

> Why in tones almost deafening
> The unlimited sorrow thunders?
>
> . . . .
>
> Back from the empty horizon
> Why does my echo come back?
> Broken, sad, and almost lost;
> Miserable like an insane woman.[53]

The narrator finds himself housing a host of pleasant memories of the past:

> There is a whole town
> Of memories in my heart;
> A whole universe of stars
> In this blue emptiness.[54]

and proceeds to recall some of them with a poignant clarity:

> The Moon seemed to be smiling
> When I first saw you.[55]
> Drinking the wine of your breasts
> Breathing the air of your exhaustion
> I would get up washing my face
> With the moonlight from your face.[56]

He starts with a catalogue of sorrows and takes us on a flashback tour of the happier scenes of the lost paradise. If the verses that catalogue his sorrows tend to be somewhat sentimental, the verses devoted to the luxurious moments of the past are sensuous, real, and unabashedly concrete:

> It was the fall of leaves and plants stood blank and withered;
> The flower-beds were dry;
> Stepping on a carpet green of buds and blossoms new,

The Early Years

> Thou gleamed upon this withered bed.
> With a thin veil drawn over thy face.
> And a light radiant hidden in thy skirts.
> In the crepuscular even-tide of life
> Thou burst on me like curiosity.
> Like beauteous lightning dwelling in a cloud.
> Like a flash restless in the lightning latent.
> Like the dark lustrous pupil in the eye.
> Like light cerulean in the pupil's orb;[57]

His plight is lonely for he knows that his tale of woe is likely to be boring, but the cloud of memory has to drench itself of the last drop. When it does, he makes his peace with the universe, calm of mind passions all spent.

Both in its intensity and its sensuousness, *Tears* is a true landmark in the history of modern Hindi poetry. The snake in the grass finally comes out in the open, and the personal side of the poetic equation becomes the really important one.

"*Ansoo,*" says Bajpai, "is far-ahead of Prasad's earlier work. It has neither the theatrical element of *Chitradhar*, nor the sentimental romanticism of *Prem-Pathik*. It has something more profound. It is an invitation from the laboratory of real life."[58] Sahney compares it with Tennyson's *In Memoriam*.[59]

Ansoo, often compared with Goethe's *Sorrows of Young Werther,* is certainly Prasad's most popular work. Sorrow, rejection, and alienation have been the principal dimensions of the Indian experience since the Bhakti Period, and *Tears* gives memorable expression to them. In a way, it provides a personalized expression to the shattered dreams of an entire wounded civilization. It is admittedly sentimental, but it must not be forgotten that the feelings of defeat and sorrow characterize much of even contemporary Hindi poetry. The contemporary poet has refined his form and modernized his images, but he is still constrained by a cultural biography that leads, for example, Vishwanath (born 1932) to compare his father with "a conquered Everest," his mother "with an ocean of milk poisoned by poverty," his sister with "a doll made out of soiled clothes," and himself with a "kettle of water/Steaming away to vapor/Water consumed into vapor."[60]

Chapter Three

Dramatize, Dramatize, Dramatize

The Nag Campaign of Janmejay

Essentially a long lyric, *Tears,* with its thin narrative framework, pushes the lyric about as far as it can be pushed. It does all that can be done with the lyrical mode, and does it successfully. After *Tears,* Prasad concentrates his attention on the dramatic and the narrative, developing the rich dramatic narratives of *Vishakha,* and *Ajatshatru.* The main theme of this period is conflict, conflict of individuals, cultures, and societies. In his plays, he goes back to ancient Indian history to find junctures that represent sharp foci of sociocultural conflicts. In his short stories, he concerns himself with individuals caught in inescapable traps; in his novel, he takes up social conflict. The lyricist in him continues to express himself in the lyrics in the plays, though his interests get wider and his concerns more encompassing.

The first product of the quest for dramatic authenticity beyond the individual's own private concerns is *The Nag Campaign of Janmejay,* first published in 1926. It is a dramatization of the conflict between Brahmans and Ksatriyas during the epic period. Janmejay, according to the *Mahabharat,* succeeded his father, Pariksit. Prasad reconstructs a considerably detailed picture of his reign from various Sanskrit sources and strives to present an authentic picture of contemporary society. The plot of this play, he says in the preface, is related to a very memorable ancient incident. He insists on its historicity and adds that "in this play, only four or five characters are imaginary." He admits having taken some liberties, but, he insists, "not more than can be taken in writing a historical play."[1]

The play opens with a dialogue between Sarama, the Aryan wife of the Nag chief Vasuki, and Manasa, Vasuki's sister. Sarama, though married to a Nag, is forced to leave the tribe for she finds her sister-in-law's bitterness toward Aryans unbearable. She moves to Indraprastha, where her son is beaten up by Janmejay's kin. When she approaches the ruler, she is labeled a traitor and receives ridicule instead of justice.

In the meanwhile Janmejay finds out that his father was killed by Taksak with the help of his own chief priest Kashyap. He vows to destroy the Nagas. Unfortunately, he kills a Brahman accidentally and is called upon to perform an elaborate ritual of penance. Although he was absolved of his sin by the victim, the Brahman community insists on his paying the traditional price. He starts preparing for his penance, but the Nagas, helped by Kashyap, disrupt his activities. He is able to defeat them but they do not give up. Kashyap advises them to abduct the queen.

The queen's kidnapping by the Nagas throws Janmejay into a rage. The fire prepared for the ritual penance becomes the cremation fire for the Nagas, and the Brahmans, for their part in the queen's kidnapping, are ordered to leave the kingdom.

The son of Janmejay's victim, however, asks that Janmejay stop the genocide as a price for having killed a Brahman. Janmejay is obliged to accept the offer and the Naga leaders vow to live peacefully with the Aryans. The informal treaty is reinforced by Janmejay's marriage to Manimala, the Naga princess.

Janmejay, even more than *Ajatshatru* and *Rajyashri,* clearly establishes Prasad as a new authentic dramatist. It is, like *Rajyashri,* a powerful character study of its protagonist. Janmejay has a strong sense of justice and although willing to abide by the rules cannot be pushed too far. He is willing to make whatever concessions tradition requires to be made for Brahmans and he is always polite with them, but when his chief priest instigates a conspiracy that leads to the kidnapping of his wife, he does not hesitate to exercise his regal powers.

He is kind and generous within the boundaries fixed by the tradition he is supposed to uphold. He saves a poor Brahman student from the satirical scrutiny of his chief priest and offers generous praise for his chief enemy's daughter. He is less than kind to Sarama when she approaches him but at that time he does not know of the less than moral conduct of the pillars of Brahmanism in his empire. At the beginning of the play, he equates holding up the tradition with dispensing justice. But when he finds out that the tradition is really nothing more than a facade to hide the greed and less than honorable motives of his allegedly selfless Brahman political advisers, he is willing to exploit his traditional privileges to expose their hypocrisy and exile them from his empire.

When the Brahmans attempt to rationalize their part in the kidnapping, he silences them: "Shut up! Aren't you ashamed of yourself? You do this and you call yourselves Brahmans!"[2] and tells them in no uncertain terms: "You'll have to pay for this. My blood is boiling. The appropriate punishment is to put you all in this fire; but, no, I am going to punish you another way. Go, leave my country. From now on, no Ksatriya king will ever perform rituals prescribed by you. This country does not need priests like you anymore. Go, you are all exiled."[3]

Having exposed the pettiness of the guardians of wisdom, he is willing to listen to the voice of reason and politely accepts the request to stop the bloodshed. Rising above the factionalism not only permitted but also promoted by Brahmans and his personal motive of revenge, Janmejay carves out a synthesis that even contemporary India could find useful.

The play is really an attack on ritual-ridden Brahmanism and the abuse of power and privilege by individual Brahmans. Taksak understands this greed and is able to exploit Kashyap. He even tells Kashyap what he thinks of the rituals presided over by

Brahmans. When he is getting ready to kill a sleeping monk, Kashyap tells him that he is frightening. Taksak's response constitutes one of the most damaging evaluations of Brahmanism: "My dear priest, when you act out your religion and when you prepare your sacrificial rituals, I find you equally frightening. When the helpless look in an animal's eye makes you feel happy, the truly religious man is frightened."[4]

Kashyap's attempt to defend himself by saying that these sacrificial rituals are a matter of duty provoke Taksak to expose the hopeless morality of the pretentious Brahman: "But we uncivilized inhabitants of the forest think that religion is something kind and generous, above and beyond our own nature. We don't mix our own weaknesses and our necessities with it. We keep our religion simple as a child's smile. We call sin 'Sin': we do masquerade it as 'religion.' "[5]

The numerous crimes and sins committed by Kashyap under the name of religion and tradition provide more than sufficient data to confirm Taksak's hypothesis. In his own way, he represents a noble and brave tribe, equal in moral and physical strength to the tribe of Janmejay. Although he takes up the Brahman offer to help him, he does not confuse personal quest for power with religion. Ironically, the guardians of morality and religion turn out to be only traders in corruption, lies, and intrigues. Given the nature of their moral strength, it is only natural that they agree to coexist. That they let the self-styled political advisers continue to exist is a further tribute to their inherent generosity.

Janmejay, a play of conflicts, is as much about the struggle for political power between the Aryans and the Nagas and the Ksatriyas and the Brahmans as it is about the struggle between the individual and tradition, and consequently about the freedom of will. As a matter of fact, the question is explicitly raised by Janmejay: "What is man? Follower of nature and slave of Fate or only a toy for it to play with? Then why does he consider himself important?"[6]

The accidental victim of his arrow also reminds him before he dies not to forget that man does not really have much of an independent will. Janmejay raises the same question again when Utank is exhorting him to avenge the killing of his father.

The tradition that forces Janmejay to order genocide and to exile Brahmans, ironically, also forces him to stop the genocide and to withdraw his order exiling Brahmans from his empire. Brought up to be a king, he knows what the limits are and when he acts against the Brahmans he knows he is within his rights. What could have been a revolutionary act is ironically presided over by Vyas, another priest. Whatever Janmejay does is politically sound and worthy of a king, but that is precisely the point. He knows what it means to be a king, a role his traditional upbringing must have familiarized him with. His anger stops short of being moral indignation, for he is as much a part of the order of the contemporary universe as those he has to fight. To say that he acts as a king and not as an individual following moral imperatives is not to take anything away from him; it simply underlines the fact that freedom of will may be as much a myth for the king as for his people.

Although *Janmejay* seems to endorse the theory that claims that freedom of will is an illusion, it is not a plea for fatalism. Free or not, the point of *Janmejay* is, man must act as he sees fit. Man may, in other words, not be free to will but he is certainly free to act as he will. Janmejay acts as he wills, though what he wills is largely dictated by his role as ruler of a reasonably well-defined universe. Janmejay's life is, says Gupta, an answer to the question he raises.[7]

There is a kind of inevitability about the events of this play. The outrage of the polite and tradition-bound king, the hypocrisy of the chief priest, the peaceful conclusion that follows the mass slaughter, and the appearance of the voice of reason in a play that seems to be controlled by irrational and emotional people all seem appropriate. What could have turned into a series of melodramatic scenes at the hands of a lesser playwright actually turns out to be a powerful play which packs a lot of action and conflict in its ninety-seven pages.

The plot of *Janmejay* is, though full of intrigues, fairly straightforward as compared to that of *Ajatshatru,* the earlier, more ambitious play. Its language is less artificial, and it is certainly better structured than *Ajatshatru.*

Kamana

The quest for dramatic perfection continues in *Kamana* (1926), a prelude, in a number of ways, to the epic *Kamayani.* Both deal with Man and his relationship to the universe around him, tracing his evolution back to the deepest recesses of prehistory. The characters of *Kamana* are simple, almost allegorical, but their simplicity, as pointed out by Gupta, is made more than credible.[8] Sumana considers it to be "the most faithful representative of Prasad's dramatic cannon."[9] Whereas *Ajatshatru* and *Janmejay* deal with the rise and fall of Buddhism, *Kamana* deals with the rise and fall of human civilization. It is an allegorical play about the loss of paradise.

It deals with the introduction of sin, wealth, and morality in the Island of Flowers, the inhabitants of which lead what can only be described as an amoral life. They work hard, help each other, and are at complete peace with nature. They live the way they do, not because they think they are supposed to but because that is the only way they know. Their language has no words for lying, wealth, dishonesty, crime, sin, and punishment, nor does it have their antonyms. Jealousy, envy, and hatred are unknown. Women are free to choose their men and there is no ruler.

This paradise is disturbed by the arrival of a handsome young man, Vilas, from the other side of the island. He captures the imagination of Kamana, a beautiful young woman. She falls in love with him, but he is more interested in ruling over the natives. In order to accomplish his goal, he introduces the concepts of wealth, responsibility, morality, and sin. He leads the natives, with the help of Kamana, down the path of greed, possession, and eventually almost total disaster. There is some opposition, but the constant supply of liquor introduced by Vilas keeps the opposition numbed. Things go the way Vilas wants them to, but eventually he is caught in his own trap and finds that he can no longer respond to the innocent love offered him by his constant companion. The loss of human sensibility, however, makes him only more ambitious. The play ends with Vilas trying to escape and Kamana and her people trying to return to their old ways.

Vilas and the natives of the Island of Flowers represent two distinctively different views regarding the nature of our universe. The difference is clearly brought out in the following dialogue between Vilas and Viveka, who never accepts the values introduced by Vilas:

Vilas: "There is a God, and he watches over us all. He rewards good deeds, and punishes evil. He dispenses justice: good for good and evil for evil."

Viveka: "But, young man, we always considered Him our father. We don't do anything evil. We simply play. And there is no punishment for play. What is this 'justice' and 'injustice'? What is a sin and what is a good deed, we do not know? We simply play, and help each other play. What does justice have to do with it? The Father watches his children play. Why should He be mad?"[10]

Vilas attributes Viveka's complaint to the latter's ignorance. When Vilas tells him that there is a distinction between good and evil, Viveka is confused: "Nothing is prohibited for us. We act the only way we know how to, and the way we act is good for us."[11]

Viveka is not the only one. The entire population has trouble understanding the alien notions Vilas introduces in order to explain his point of view. He asks two of the natives to promise that they will never tell anyone that they had seen a lot of gold at his place. They do, but Vilas wants to be reassured that they are not lying. Leela is confused, for she does not understand what he wants:

Vilas:	"You are not lying, are you?"
Leela:	"What is 'lying'?"
Vilas:	"Not doing what one says one will."
Kamana:	"But we never do that."[12]

That Vilas has to paraphrase a common expression of his language underlines the utter simplicity of the natives.

The paraphrases given by Vilas sometimes contain disarming ironic twists that in a less innocent world such as the audience's cannot go undetected:

Vinod:	"What's a prison?"
Vilas:	"Oh, that's where you keep criminals. It's the strength of an empire and its chief weapon."[13]

The exchange system, yellow gold for red blood, introduced by Vilas makes the natives not only kill each other but also want to take over other peoples. They multiply their needs so much that they have to attack others in order to maintain themselves. This, as Viveka points out, creates a rather strange sense of justice. When the killers of one of the natives are brought to justice, Viveka cannot refrain from observing: "I have never seen anything like this before. It is incredible. They killed someone for gold but you are collectively going to kill innocent people in order to maintain yourselves."[14]

Viveka comprehends the real nature of war and goes out to seek the help of an enemy alien to help him fight the real enemy: "There is a new Kingdom in our country and mine. It is owned by a group of our enemies. It has become the guardian of torture. Do we want to save ourselves from it?"[15]

Vilas succeeds to the extent he does because he follows the principle discovered by him very early in the play: "If you want to become the ruler, you have to make them sinners. A people that is not burdened with crime and sin, can never accept the rule of one of their own, much less of an alien."[16] The idea of sin may or may not be a theological necessity, but it certainly is a political necessity, at least for the ruling class.

Kamana is a commentary on the human decision to abandon the somewhat limited pleasures of living in unison with nature in favor of the newer modes of pleasure offered by the world of golden industry. Kamana is fascinated by the ever increasing means of pleasure: "I have been straightened out. My pride is gone. He came as a guest, but is now the lord. This moonlight is making the universe one. The stream of pleasure is flowing. . . . Vilas! your presence has filled my mind with ideas of new pleasure giving devices."[17]

The problem is that the search inaugurated by Vilas has no end. It makes it impossible to stop till the pursuer is consumed by what is pursued. Vilas, the advocate of wealth, time, and leisure, is drowned because the boat he attempts to escape in is loaded with gold. The pursuit of wealth allows the natives to create new industries and institutions but they all turn into meaningless exercises. When one of the natives arrives arrested in the newly created city, he is asked to wait till he has been interrogated by a justice of the peace. His response is to ask why they need a justice of the peace when they have no peace.[18]

That the play is also intended as a scathing evaluation of colonialism should be obvious. The simple people of the Island of Flowers are seduced by gold and the new system of values Vilas brings with him. The introduction of the vocabulary of sin creates new distinctions that make it possible for the colonizer to rule and to dispense "justice." The language of sin is, however, easy to learn and when the natives have learned it they cannot avoid using it against the Prospero that brought it with him. His boat is capsized and the Calibans decide to become their own masters once more. That they will ever go back to the paradise they left behind is uncertain, but the question may well be irrelevant.

The play presents a simple and forceful picture of the corruption and decline of a people. Although the characters are intended as allegorical figures, they are not reduced to mere symbolic entities.

The simple Kamana, the clever Vilas, and the wise Viveka all come out as real human beings, trying to resolve the allegorical conflicts they represent very much in personal, dramatic terms.

The play is, however, a bit too ambitious. In spite of its simple language and many strengths, it does not quite come off. Prasad tries to do a bit too much in attempting to telescope the entire history of human civilization within the framework of an allegorical play.

Rajyashri Revisited

Apparently realizing that he had undertaken a bit too much in *Kamana,* the concerns of which remain constantly with him till they are tackled again in *Kamayani,* he returns to a more manageable conflict, the one he had depicted in one of his earliest historical plays, *Rajyashri,* a revised edition of which was also published in 1927.

Whereas the 1915 edition contains only thirty-nine pages, the revised edition contains seventy pages. Prasad added a whole act and a few scenes. Apart from making the play more substantial, he also made some important stylistic changes. Whereas the first edition contains some dialogues in verse, the revised edition is entirely in prose. The revised edition, according to Bahri, is far more satisfying and mature.[19]

The addition of the character of Vikat Ghosh allows the dramatist to introduce wit and humor as integral parts of the play. Although both *Gentleman* and *Penance* contain humor, *Rajyashri* marks, according to Gupta, the beginning of the use of polished dramatic wit:[20]

Mudhukar:	"A guest this late!"
Vikat Ghosh:	"I shall leave soon."
Mudhukar:	"Yes, no point in troubling yourself too much. You have to go far, don't you?"
Vikat Ghosh:	"Be quiet. You haven't even asked me why I came here."
Mudhukar:	"You go ahead, leave. I'll find out later."[21]

The revised edition also introduces the lyrical romanticism of *Tears* through the character of Surma, the flower-girl. She sings two songs that could have been independent lyrics: "Hope Is Disappointed, the Soul Remains Thirsty" and "How Does One Take Care of Love?"

The character of Harshavardhan, merely an outline in the background in the first edition, is sketched out more fully in a couple of entirely new scenes of the revised edition. Although some critics feel that the added emphasis on Harshavardhan creates a conflict of focus, Rajyashri undoubtedly remains the chief figure of the revised edition.[22] The more fully spelled out character of Harshavardhan only adds to her presence in the play.

"Whatever is dramatic and attractive in *Rajyashri*," observes Gupta, "is added later; whatever is dull, is there from before. Whatever has been added is appropriate for this age."[23] The revised version is, according to Bhatnagar, "a supreme delineation of contemporary culture and a notable piece of dramaturgy."[24]

Skandgupta

His next play, *Skandgupta,* deals with the declining years of the Gupta empire, which was being torn apart by trivial, and utterly selfish, internal strife. The decadence of the empire in general is counterpointed against Skandgupta, "the shield of the Aryavrata."[25]

The play has a focus: Skandgupta, who, according to Joshi, "saved India from having to change its history and geography."[26] The playwright has a sharply defined aim: to depict contemporary conditions authentically and to make Skandgupta credible in sorting out the decadent mess all around him. The problem, often raised in connection with *Ajatshatru,* as to who is the protagonist does not arise here for the answer is perfectly obvious. There are no multiplicities in *Skandgupta*: there is one protagonist, there is one problem and there are no side-tracking subplots. It is undoubtedly one of Prasad's finest dramatic efforts.

The first words of *Skandgupta,* as rightly pointed out by Gupta,[27] sum up not only the character of Skandgupta, the reluctant emperor who is primarily a soldier, but also the forces he has to defeat: "How empty and intoxicating is power! The wish to be the decision maker harnesses it to do absurd things."[28]

Based on historical facts, the play begins with a description of the crisis-ridden kingdoms of the Gupta empire, currently under attack by Hunas and unable to fight back because of corruption and a general moral decline.[29] The ambassador of Malava comes seeking help, which is provided by Skandgupta. The Shakas and the Hunas are defeated and taken prisoners.[30] Later, Skandgupta has to leave for Magadha, a hotbed of dirty domestic intrigues. For his services, Skandgupta is offered the princedom of Malava. The intrigues and attacks, however, seem endless, and Skandgupta has to defeat the barbarian attackers once again. Another inside betrayal causes him to lose a large number of his soldiers while chasing the Hunas. Exhausted by these endless power games, Skandgupta is almost ready to give up his efforts, but has to fight another battle against the Hunas, defeating them once more. Their leader is taken prisoner, but later released on the condition that he stay on the other side of Sindh. The play ends with Devasena requesting permission to leave. Skandgupta's response and Devasena's comments on it remind the viewer of the opening words of the play, uttered by the soldier emperor, who really never expected very much for himself.

Skandgupta: "The spring of this garden, the princess of this fairyland, the Minerva of this Olympus, how can I say that you can leave? (With pause and hesitation) And how can I possibly try to stop you? Devasena! You go. The unfortunate Skandgupta must be alone."

Devasena: "Pain is the touchstone of life, and fire a mechanism for trial. You have to be able to do that, Emperor! Every time-bound pleasure has an end. Endless pleasure is not worth pursuing. In this life, you have been my god; in the next, you will be mine. But for now, you have to excuse me!"[31]

Dramatize, Dramatize, Dramatize

Skandgupta, engaged in the mysterious activities of helping an empire, only, according to his admission, because of the inescapable name he has inherited, is the proverbial Aryan hero, handsome, serious, calm, unselfish, and modest. Apparently subscribing to the theory of Karma, though he has his bouts of inaction of the type that inflicted Arjuna on the battlegrounds of the *Mahabharata* and that inspired Krishna's famous dramatic lecture against inaction, *The Bhagavad Gita,* Skandgupta does better precisely because he is not interested in personal rewards.[32] He does get the reward, of course, as the theory would predict, but he never consciously seeks it.

It is, of course, possible to argue that Skandgupta is really not that uninterested, for he talks and behaves like an emperor: "Skandgupta alone is prepared to protect Malava. Go, and sleep without fear. As long as Skandgupta is alive, no harm will come to Malava."[33]

Argal raises the question of whether Skandgupta is a hypocrite and provides a plausible defense against an affirmative answer.[34] He argues that Skandgupta's paramount concern is the integrity of the empire and he is unwilling to add to the numerous intrigues that already exist by provoking his admirers to put another one into action on his behalf. The net result: he is not uninterested in accepting the role he knows he is fully capable of, but he is certainly not going to seek it. When the crown is virtually thrown at his feet, he gracefully accepts it, like a true prince, and conducts himself in a manner that can only shame the petty power seekers all around him.

Drama and conflict are almost synonymous terms, and *Skandgupta* is full of of conflict, both internal and external. The internal conflict is essentially in the mind of Skandgupta himself, constantly debating the ultimate worth of the role he knows he is not only fit for but also destined to assume: "Why should I bear the burden of this empire? I am not at peace. All because I exist. It seems that I am the only hope, yet the world would have gone on without me. But I have nothing to gain."[35]

Skandgupta turns down not only Vijaya's offer of help but also

Vijaya, the woman he loves, for she would have him use petty means:

Skandgupta: "Be quiet, Vijaya. This is the land I worship, and I would not have you corrupt it with your intrigues. Even if you could get me heaven, I would not want it."
Vijaya: "I still have two treasure-houses. You can collect your own armies and defeat the Hunas."
Skandgupta: "But I cannot sell myself for an empire. Vijaya, please leave. There is no need for this shameful demonstration. Let this story end here."[36]

Skandgupta's internal conflict is matched by Devasena's. She loves him desperately, but refuses to indulge either in intrigue or in blatantly selfish demonstrations. She accepts her fate with a dignity that only Skandgupta can match, and it is only befitting that the play ends with both Devasena and Skandgupta rising, once more, above themselves, calm of mind, passions spent.

There is, as should be obvious by now, plenty of external conflict in the play, prince against prince, ministers against the king, Hunas against the empire, and the principalities of the empire against each other. These conflicts keep the play moving, unlike *Ajatshatru,* which seems to falter. *Skandgupta* is a rather long play, but the length is never quite felt. Although *Skandgupta* has a large cast, characters other than Skandgupta are measurably minor. Most of them serve to highlight the character of Skandgupta. Though well drawn, they are never allowed to get out of hand. Keeping them in place provides *Skandgupta* with the sharpness in focus, conspicuously lacking in *Ajatshatru*.

Skandgupta, like all his plays, contains quite a few songs, but they never seem to be merely purple lyrical interludes, added for their own sake, as alleged by Shukla.[37] Gupta examines each song in the play to show its relevance and his arguments are convincing.[38] *Skandgupta* is a play of conflict, patriotism, love, and sorrow, and the songs reflect these concerns. The sun, for example, blesses India, in one of the songs of the last act, by "Presenting it with first rays in the playground of the Himalayas."[39]

The language of *Skandgupta* is refined, and not pseudopoetic. It is almost entirely prose. The dialogue is crisp. There are occasional soliloquies and bits of philosophizing, but they all seem more than dramatically justified, like the speech of Skandgupta, already quoted above, in which he examines his own motives and the meaning of the role he seems to be destined for.

Skandgupta, the culmination of the experiment begun with *Vishakha,* is, according to most Hindi critics, quite easily the best of his plays. While *Vishakha* and *Janmejay* announce the arrival of a new dramatic style in Hindi and *Ajatshatru* establishes that style as unmistakable, *Skandgupta* puts the final seal of excellence on that style, henceforth to be followed and talked about. Hindi drama before Prasad has very little to offer; after him, there has been a deluge of playwrights, and Prasad has always been the measure of their success.

One Sip

Both *Ajatshatru* and *Skandgupta* are long plays, much too long, according to some. The next play, *One Sip* [*Ek Ghunt*], is not only short, but also the first one-act play of Hindi. It was first published in 1929. The publisher's preface concludes: "Within the tradition of one-act plays *Ek Ghunt* is the first one-act play of Hindi literature. In this humorous and ironical one-act play, Prasad symbolically expresses his principles of *anandvad* in a very deft manner. Opening with the conflict between free love and married love, the play concludes with a happy medium. That one sip of *anand* is what is needed, is obviously the message of the play."[40]

The play exposes the selfish motives underlying the facile rhetoric of Anand, a self-styled advocate of free love. He finds that Vanlata's love is not returned by her poet husband, and tries to seduce her by attracting her by his apparently innocent rhetoric. She, however, sees through the rhetoric:

Anand: "Since I don't dislike anybody, I love everybody. I am entitled to love."

Vanlata: "Of course not, because I don't love you. Your love means nothing to me."

Anand: "Then! (biting his lips)"

Vanlata: "Then this (thinking a little) that the one I love, and only he, should love me, my heart, my body, to see me satisfied. No saturation, but a sharing: he drinks a little, and I a little. Understand? And that has no place for your hollow philosophy and your empty rhetoric."

Anand: (Covering up a bit) "I am a traveller and this world is a path. Each one is following his own route. Call it what you like, a minute, an age, or a life. It is simply a moment. You rest a bit and then you leave again. That's why unattached love is possible. Share your drink with everyone—that's my message."

Vanlata: "You are trying to seduce me with your rhetoric."[41]

Anand is made to see that the free, unattached love he so fervently advocates is probably only a linguistic game, for love requires commitment and commitments are binding. He accepts a drink offered by Premlata and the "strings" attached with it.

Quite obviously a problem play, *One Sip* is, unfortunately, treated unjustly by most admirers of Prasad, partly because it does not have the high seriousness of his other plays and partly because the problem it deals with appears to these critics not to have any cosmic consequences. Admittedly a light piece, *One Sip*, however, deserves better. It is a play of irony, a quality rarely appreciated by the philosophically minded Hindi critics of Prasad. The play is also more realistic.

One Sip is, however, far removed from the dramatic height achieved in *Skandgupta*. That level of artistic sophistication is achieved by Prasad only through the help of ancient Indian history. He apparently felt more comfortable with the past, which helps him to repeat the excellence of *Skandgupta* in his next highly regarded classic *Chandragupta*, first published in 1931.

Chapter Four
Some More Fiction
The Lighthouse

With the exception of *One Sip,* the period between the publication of *Skandgupta* and his next major play *Chandragupta* is devoted to short fiction and a novel.

The Skeleton [*Kankal*], a novel, and *The Lighthouse* [*Akash Deep*] and *The Storm* [*Andhi*], collections of short stories, were published in 1929.

His short stories are all very dramatic in nature, and many of them can be, with the simple addition of a few stage directions, converted into one-act plays, the genre exploited in *One Sip.* Intense dramatic conflict is their major ingredient. Most of them, like his plays, deal with the past, which he takes pains to reconstruct authentically. They are written in a language that frequently approaches the lyrical. In a way, his short stories represent a perfect combination of his lyrical and dramatic talents with his love of ancient Indian history.

Some of his best short stories are to be found in *The Lighthouse*, a collection of nineteen short stories written between 1926 and 1929. It contains some of the most powerful and original short stories in Hindi. The story after which the collection is named is regarded by many as one of the best short stories in Hindi. It deals with the tragic conflict in the mind of Champa, who loves a man she cannot trust for she thinks he may have been responsible for the death of her father. Champa and Buddhagupta meet only to part, and "The Lighthouse" ["Akash Deep"] is a moving record of what happens en route.

It opens with a dramatic encounter between Champa and Buddhagupta, both prisoners of a pirate:

"Prisoner!"
"What do you want? Let me sleep."
"Do you want to be free."
"Not right now. When I wake up. Be quiet."
"But then you won't be able to."
"It's cold. Wish somebody would find me a blanket."
"A storm seems to be building up. This is the moment. My handcuffs are loose."
"Then you are a prisoner, too?"[1]

They manage to release themselves. When they embrace each other in happiness, Buddhagupta is surprisd to find that his fellow prisoner is a woman. He expresses his surprise, only to be disarmed by Champa: " 'What is this? You are a woman?' 'Why? Is it a sin to be a woman?' "[2]

Buddhagupta leads a mutiny and takes over the ship. He becomes a very successful shipping magnate and acquires an island, which he names after Champa. Champa, however, is unwilling to become a part of his life. She cannot get rid of the suspicion that he might have killed her father.

Champa loves and hates Buddhagupta at the same time. Her ambivalence creates a dramatic tension that makes the story a real masterpiece. The complex pattern of this love-hate relationship is revealed when Champa and Buddhagupta embrace each other on the quiet island:

During the embrace, Champa cautiously took a knife out.
"Buddhagupta, I shall sink my knife of revenge in this endless water today. My heart has betrayed: it has repeatedly deceived me."
Piercing the heart of the sea, the knife disappeared. "Then, should I start trusting today? Have I been forgiven?" The sea-man asked in a voice trembling with surprise.[3]

Champa, typically, makes no apologies and hides nothing. Her answer reflects both her conflict and her strength: "Trust? Never, Buddhagupta. When I couldn't trust my heart—it betrayed me—how can I say! I hate you, but even then I can die for you. It is not fair, sea-man. I love you."[4]

Buddhagupta tries to assure her that he is not responsible for her father's death, but suspicion is a mental fact. Champa cannot accept the explanation: "Only if I could believe that, Buddhagupta! That day would have been a beautiful day and that moment a cherishable moment."[5]

Her conflict tears Buddhagupta apart: "You came into my life like a lost star, lighting a dawn in the darkness of my soul. You brought the laughter of peace and joy into a life devoted to the pursuit of power and wealth. But I couldn't laugh."[6] Unable to persuade her to accept him and unable to stay rejected, Buddhagupta leaves.

She cannot resolve the fatal doubt and resigns herself to lighting floating oil lamps, the ritual her mother used to perform while praying for her husband's security on the high sea. She takes over the ritual deliberately, praying for the man she loves but knowing full well that she could never negotiate the high sea of her doubts.

"The Lighthouse" is one of the most dramatic stories of Prasad. Its seven sections are rather like the seven acts of a play. The first act describes the encounter between two strangers; the second establishes the seaworthy credentials of Buddhagupta; the third establishes the outline of his dream when he names the newly discovered island after Champa; the fourth brings out the conflict in Champa's mind; the fifth provides a moving description of Champa's inner conflict; the penultimate one underlines the irreconcilable nature of that conflict; and the last one shows Champa's lonely existence on the remote island named after her.

It is also one of his most poetic stories. Its rich and evocative language captures the beauty of the isolated island where Champa and Buddhagupta are engaged in sorting out their destinies with a typically Prasadian picturesqueness: "Right in front was the silver collection of water coins. The waves were busy making diamonds and sapphires for the nymphs of Varuna. Like mysterious fairies, they appeared only to create the music of laughter and then to disappear. Champa saw the slightly puzzled shadow of her chandelier in the wet treasury of water! It went around a hundred times to complete itself."[7]

Strong and beautiful, Champa is a self-conscious and self-confident woman. She knows that she loves Buddhagupta, but also knows her inability to cope with the doubt that he may have killed her father. The lonely existence she chooses for herself is an inevitable consequence of her decision to define her existence in terms of doubting. She, however, does not solicit any pity. She knows what she is doing. Hers is an honest struggle, carried out to its logical conclusion. She asks for no sympathy and no tears.

Buddhagupta is also a strong character. He asks for love, actually begs for it. But when the inevitability of an unhappy conclusion becomes obvious to him, he leaves, sad and broken-hearted, but still willing to risk the adventure of life.

There are no unnatural deaths and no suicides in "The Lighthouse." Champa dies a natural death at the end of her long, lonely journey. Both Champa and Buddhagupta fight out the ironies of their existence, providing a rich, tragic record of human experience that has the awe-inspiring sadness and power of a real tragedy.

Champa dies on an unknown island, and the only monument erected to commemorate the memory of her conflict is "The Lighthouse." Prasad erects another such monument in "Mamata" in the memory of an unknown Brahman widow who once gave refuge to Humayun, the Moghul emperor.[8]

"Mamata" is the story of a young Brahman widow who runs away from her father's house to live a lonely existence in a small hut in Sarnath, where Buddha gave his first sermons. One night, while reading, she is interrupted: " 'Mother! I need shelter.' 'Who are you?' asked the woman. 'I am a Moghul, I am running away from Shershah. I am unable to walk any more.' "[9]

She is caught on the horns of a dilemma: her religion tells her to provide shelter to anyone seeking it, but the man asking for shelter happens to belong to a religion the followers of which killed her father. She tells him to go away, but only to revise her decision and to invite him in: "Go in, you tired and afraid traveler! Whosoever you are, I give you shelter. I am a Brahman girl. Even if others don't follow their religion, why should I abandon it?"[10]

The next morning Moghul armies seek out Humayun. They look for Mamata, but cannot find her. Humayun leaves instructions that a house should be built there. A few years later, a house is built with a commemorative stone that reads: "The emperor of seven nations Humayun rested here for a day. His son Akbar ordered this sky-scraping temple made in his memory."[11] The story concludes with the comment that Mamata's name was not to be found anywhere on that stone.

The unsung heroes and heroines of ancient and not so ancient Indian history provide the materials for many of Prasad's historical short stories. He takes plausible incidents and conflicts and builds a rich picture of the glory that was India. The pride and conflict of Champa and Mamata, the really human needs of a defeated Humayun, and the partially sentimental gesture of Akbar all contribute to a very successful reconstruction of the social life of the forgotten days of Indian history.

Integrity and self-pride are, in fact, the hallmarks of the major characters of most of these short stories. The central character of "The Beggar Woman" ["Bhikarin"], for example, does not allow those whose charity her life depends on to walk over her. "The Beggar Woman" is a powerful story in which the helpless sentimentalism of a middle-class youth is counterpointed against the tough self-pride of a beggar. Nirmal goes with his mother for a ceremonial religious dip in the Ganges. There they meet a young beggar woman. Nirmal tries to persuade his mother to employ her, but she turns her down because she does not know anything about her caste. Nirmal's brilliant argument that "all the poor come from the same caste" falls on the ritualistic deaf ears of his mother. The incident is repeated when he goes out with his sister-in-law. The beggar women is there again. Nirmal gets into an argument with his sister-in-law and tells her that he would even consider marrying the beggar. The beggar woman finds all this argumentation too much and speaks up: "You couldn't give me a penny in two days, then why do you abuse me? Marrying someone like me is a long shot, Sir."[12]

Nirmal's mother represents the ritual-ridden social structure satirized in *The Skeleton* and he the helpless young product of the joint-family system. His idealism is a linguistic game, his mother's religiosity a facade. There is really not much to choose between the two. The rich and the aware are left playing their game as the beggar woman disappears, singing. The story provides a satirical glimpse of the rut sometimes described as Indian culture.

The central characters of most of the stories of *The Lighthouse* are, like Champa, strong women who fight for their rights as individuals. Sometimes they even fight back with a vengeance. "Echo" ["Pratidhwani"] is a good example. It is the story of Tara, who is made to feel responsible for the death of her husband, and Shyama, an orphan of fourteen. Tara fights the insinuation that she was responsible for her husband's death and Shyama does not hesitate to attack the dying Prakash, a decadent lecher.

Even more impressive, both in her character and in her tactics, is Vilasini, the central figure of "The Bangle Woman" ["Churiwali"]. Vilasini finds it difficult to live with the fact that she cannot have an ordinary married life just because her mother was a prostitute. In a culture that provides for no rehabilitation centers, she sets out to rehabilitate herself, with angelic innocence that has a cutting edge.

She sets her eyes on Vijay Krisna, a local landed aristocrat, and becomes a door-to-door saleslady, selling goods to rich women, particularly to the wife of Vijay Krisna. She succeeds in attracting the man of her choice, but for him she was only a diversion from the routine life of a married aristocrat.

He loses his fortune and decides to go back to remanaging his estate. She offers her wealth, but is turned down for reasons she finds incomprehensible because she defines her relationship with him in entirely different terms:

"But why are you worried? I am yours, and so is my wealth."
Vijay Krishna replied, "I cannot allow a prostitute to maintain me."
Her dream of becoming a bride is shattered: "I can't be a bride! Does society have no alternative for people like me? Even after the price I have paid!"[13]

She cannot understand why she could not share the joys of ordinary life with the wife of Vijay Krishna. She cannot understand why Vijay Krishna treated her the way he did.

The Lighthouse abounds in scenes of intense dramatic conflict. Virtually every story in the collection is a crossroads. The characters in these stories seem to meet only for brief encounters at these crossroads. Their meeting point calls for a decision, and more often than not they go their separate ways. The encounters, however, produce short stories haunting in their dramatic intensity.

The nature and structure of these encounters is best exemplified in "The Recluse" ["Vairagi"], the shortest and perhaps the most intense story in the collection. Its two and a half pages contain more drama than some five-act plays. The self-imposed isolation of a lonely recluse is broken by a young woman asking for refuge. The recluse, visibly shaken, welcomes the guest.

The necessary formality of conversation produces the following dialogue:

The woman said, "Having turned down the world of gold, the admiration of a son, the affection of a mother, the pleasure of fame, and the glory of power, how could you be attached to this little piece of land? Why so much work? What for?"
"Only for guests like you. When someone is turned out of a palace, he finds refuge in a spot like this. I feel happy when someone used to a soft bed finds this earth comforting."
"How long do you propose to continue it?"
"*Ad infinitum,* I hope."[14]

Having started on a note such as this, there is hardly any place for exchanging pleasantries. Argument is carried out to its logical and psychological extreme:

> "How long is your shelter good for?"
> "Till there is another one."
> "I have none, nor am I likely to find one."
> "For life?"—Surprised, the recluse asked.
> "Yes."[15]

The monosyllabic "Yes" presses for the ultimate decision and the recluse buys a few seconds by asking the guest if she is cold. She says "Yes" and he lights a fire, apparently using every extra second at his disposal.

The primitive fire, however, does not take long to start and the players in this intense psychological drama are soon back to conclude the act:

> "How long are you going to stay out?"
> "I'll leave after the night is over. Find another shelter. It won't be good to stay here. Why should I come in just for the night?"[16]

The forthrightness of the guest pulls the rug from beneath the host's feet. But he recovers and tells the guest that she can live there freely. Her response really forces the host to make an existential decision: "You are attached to this hut. I shall not make you fear that I want to share it with you."[17] And he does. " 'Someone is calling me, take care of the hut!'—said the recluse, disappearing into the darkness. The woman was left alone."[18]

That the drama was not merely staged for a show of strength but for something far more profound is indicated by the narrator's concluding comment: "Travellers noted that a yellow face in that hut was always anxiously waiting for someone to return."[19]

The host realizes his dream of detachment, but loses human love; the guest wins the moral argument, but loses the pleasures of human attachment. The choice has to be made, and they both make it. "The Recluse" is the story of one such choice. It is more of an epiphany than a short story. Two strangers reenact the climax of human drama and the story captures the essence of their deadly serious play. There are no redundancies in "The Recluse." The decisions that matter are instinctive and made in split seconds. "The Recluse" is a replay of one such split second.

The Storm

Written in a similar vein, *The Storm* reconfirms Prasad's mastery of the medium. It contains eleven short stories, most of them devoted to simple, but profound, human conflicts.

"Madhua," considered one of the best pieces in the collection, is the story of a drunkard who willingly spends his last dollar to feed a hungry child and eventually ends up reforming himself in order to take care of him. The change, however, is not a sentimental, melodramatic change of heart, but a realization of the potential subtle sensitivity that drives the drunkard to drink:

Your highness! I cannot help remembering the stories of the golden days of our aristocracy, of the despair of the poor, and of the slow death of the princesses. Their pain is mine, and I drink to forget it. The rich become poor. The proud lose their pride. Even then the world continues to be insane. It is to forget its insanity that I drink, your highness! Otherwise, why would anyone want to get hooked on something like this?[20]

It is not entirely without conflict that he accepts his new responsibility. It is for the first time, he tells us, that he has to think of feeding another mouth, and he is irritated by it. After getting a tip from his employer, he runs to the street to buy himself half a bottle of country liquor, but reconsiders his decision:

What about this boy? I've got to feed him. What's he going to eat and how much? Damn it! I have never had to think about feeding someone else before. What should I get? Let me first get myself half a bottle. But he found himself in front of a store selling candies. He forgot his half bottle and bought some candies. He picked up some snacks also. He almost ran home and put the stuff before the child, who was delighted to see it. The expression on the child's face made him smile.[21]

The final conflict comes when Madhua refuses to go back to his slave-driving employer and firmly confirms his intentions to stay with the drunkard, although the latter has just been thrown out of his tenement:

"Can you sleep under a tree?"
"I can stay anywhere, but I won't go back to my previous employer."
The drunkard stared at him. The child's eyes were swearing determination.
He said to himself: "What did I do to get stuck with him! Now, I can't drink again."[22]

"Madhua" is a compelling story almost totally devoid of sentimentalism. It is a story of human concern in which the pathetic and the marginal play a role that makes the real and the central appear less than human. Although the story provides enough opportunities to moralize, Prasad carefully abstains from it. The incidents are narrated with an objectivity that invites the reader to be right in the center of things.

Perhaps the best piece in the collection is "Reward" ["Puruskar"], similar both in design and execution to "The Lighthouse." It deals with the conflict generated by the divided loyalties of Madhulika, who helps her king arrest the man she loves because he has unscrupulous plans to acquire power.

Chiefly concerned with the inevitable conflict generated by divided loyalties, the story also seeks to capture the glory of ancient India: "Chariots, elephants, and horses lined up. There was no shortage of spectators. The elephant sat down, and the king stepped down the ladder. Married and unmarried women formed a singing procession."[23]

Some More Fiction

Madhulika falls in love with Arun, but when she finds out that Arun plans to take over power from her king, she betrays him. Arun is taken prisoner, brought to trial, and sentenced to death. Pleased with her patriotic decision to save the kingdom, the King of Koshal generously offers her crown land. But she rejects the offer:

Madhulika looked towards the prisoner, Arun, and said: "I don't want anything." Arun smiled. The King declared: "No, I have to reward you, you can ask for whatever you want."
"Then," moving towards Arun, she said, "give me death."[24]

The behavior of Madhulika may appear to be a bit mysterious. But it appears equally mysterious to the prince of Magadha when she turns him down. She offers the following explanation to the mystified prince: "This is the mystery of the human heart and not mine. If the human heart could be made to obey rules, the prince of Magadha would have been attracted to a princess and not to the daughter of a farmer."[25]

The anticlimactic climax of "Reward" is fully prepared for: it comes as an inevitable end and not as a melodramatic twist. The highly individualistic character of Madhulika incorporates it as another side of her mysterious self. It is as much a key to an understanding of the plot as it is to an understanding of Madhulika's complex sense of loyalty.

Equally complex is the character of Radha in "A Broken Vow" ("Vrat Bhang"), a story of revenge and integrity. The story begins with Nandan seeking to reestablish friendship with his old classmate Kapinjal, who feels that Nandan has ignored him once too often. Nandan's offer is turned down and Kapinjal vows to destroy him. They part, Nandan with regret and Kapinjal with revenge in his heart.

Later, Radha marries Nandan, whose father virtually worships Kapinjal, now a holy man. Kapinjal tells him that his daughter-in-law is a curse on the family. Predictably, he listens to him and threatens to drive Radha out of his palace. Radha, however, refuses to be driven out, and Nandan unfortunately goes along with his father, leaving his wife alone to fight for herself.

There is a flood and one day Nandan, having been turned out by his father, finds himself with a few refugees seeking help at the door of his wife's mansion. The help is readily granted and Radha is pleased to see her husband gather enough courage to have left his father's wealth. He goes out again to help another refugee, who turns out to be Kapinjal. Kapinjal does not want to work with Nandan but the latter convinces him that there are more important things waiting than a petty personal feud.

Although chance plays a rather heavy role in the story, its powerful characterization and dramatic intensity more than compensate for what appears to be a somewhat contrived plot. Radha is clearly the most powerful character. Like Dhruvaswamini, she accepts her role as the bride of a wealthy family, but when the head of the family wants to take away the privileges that go with that role she stands up for her rights. She is meek and submissive, polite and humble, but, when mistreated, fully capable of shaking the doll's house. Here is her confrontation with her father-in-law:

Kailash asked: "Why did you misbehave with the holy man?"

"No Father! He misbehaved: one who cannot observe common courtesy with women cannot be a holy man."

"What are you saying? You idiot. He *is* a holy man."

"If holiness is that irreligious, and religion is that shameless, then it is not for women, Father! Are you worshipping religion or fear?"

"You are certainly a curse."

"Only God knows that. Man is too insignificant to decide that. Father. . . ."

Stopping her, and with great anger Kailash said: "To let you stay here is to let misfortune stay here; you get out of this palace."

"I am not a slave. My rights can be taken away only if I am abandoned as the wife of my husband. I am, however, confident that there is nothing in my conduct so far to deprive me of my position. No one can take it away from me."[26]

Dramatic confrontations of this kind are, in fact, the highlights of the story. Here is Nandan trying to persuade Kapinjal to bury the hatchet:

"Then, you won't listen to me?"
"No, the gap between us cannot be bridged any more."
"And what happens to the friendship of the past?"
"Oh, nothing!"[27]

Most of the stories of *The Storm*, like "Reward," "A Broken Vow," "Chain," and "Madhua," deal with the complex nature of human commitments. "Chain" ["Bedi"], for example, is the story of a young boy whose blind father keeps him enchained so that he does not run away; "The Village Song" ["Gram-Geet"] and "Undying Memory" ["Amit Smriti"] deal with traumatic experiences that leave marks not to be erased. If most of them appear to be somewhat sentimental, it is only because life in general tends to be somewhat less rational, at least in the part of the world Prasad is concerned with. If poverty and lack of means loom large in these stories it is only because these things have formed an inescapable part of the human equation of post–golden-age India. What stands out, however, is not the poverty of a Gheesu, who makes a living by changing currency bills for a few cents a day, but his courage in accepting the responsibility of Bindo.

The language of these stories is flexible, dramatic, and forceful. It changes according to situation and character. Their technique is typically Prasadian. They attempt to present a slice of life and do it with an intensity at once original and unique.

Madan has correctly observed that the short stories of Prasad are dramatic in construction and poetic in conception.[28] The effort to combine the poetic, or to be more precise, the lyrical, and the dramatic is, however, not always successful, and some of his stories are really nothing more than collections of purple passages that do not hang together. But when he is able to combine the dramatic and the poetic, the results are really astonishing.

The Skeleton

His first novel, *The Skeleton* [*Kankal*], presumably written in response to Prem Chand's objection that Prasad was obsessed with the ghosts of the past, is a commentary on a society obsessed with rituals. It revolves around the story of Niranjan and Kishori. Niranjan is offered to a monastery by his parents. He later becomes its chief, but when he does, he finds it impossible to cope with the sexual temptation offered by Kishori, his boyhood friend. He runs away, but only to be asked later to bestow his divine blessings on Kishori, now married to a wealthy businessman. Kishori and her husband ask him for the gift of a son, but when the son arrives Kishori's husband abandons both the child and its mother. The son ends up as a beggar and the novel ends with the discovery of his dead body.

The plot of the novel, however, is not half as simple and straightforward as the outline above may suggest. There are numerous subplots, involving suicide, attempted suicide, adultery, illegitimate children, and overnight conversions.

Intended as a commentary on a society obsessed with rituals, *The Skeleton* is a serious effort to lay bare the moral disintegration and sexual promiscuousness of Indian society. Whereas *One Sip* makes fun of the idea of free love, *The Skeleton* counterpoints it against the meaningless ritual called marriage. One of the characters says:

Those who say that love outside of marriage is undesirable and only a disguise for lust must be mistaken. Marriage is a union of souls. I give myself to you, and you give yourself to me. Why should we need an intermediary? Why should we worry about wedding chants?"[29]

Although the views expressed in *One Sip* and *The Skeleton* may appear to be contradictory, they are not. *One Sip* exposes the exploitative potential of free love, for it can become a tool of sexual exploitation. *The Skeleton*, on the other hand, argues for the acceptance of free love that is an expression of an emotional commitment. The free love advocated by *One Sip* is a rhetorical device for seducing innocent women; the free love defended in *The Skeleton* is not a linguistic game but a sincere human concern. Whereas *The Skeleton* appears to be a diatribe against marriage, *One Sip* seems to be a defense of it. The difference, however, is only superficial. *One Sip* is a defense of marriage and *The Skeleton* is a criticism of the ritual that often only legalizes mutual torture. The sanctity of the relevant contract is defined by the partners that enter into it and not by outside agencies. Both *One Sip* and *The Skeleton* underline that personal element in the equation, and thus express what is fundamentally the same point.

The Skeleton, though predominantly a social satire, is not without some powerful descriptions of subtle psychological conflicts. When Kishori approaches Niranjan, now a monk, for the gift of a son, Niranjan finds himself caught in the conflict he thought he had left behind forever:

Kishori said: "I come here, my Lord, for a very selfish reason. I have never seen the face of a child."

Niranjan asked in a serious tone: "You are only eighteen or nineteen. Why should you be so worried about it?"[30]

Kishori felt embarrassed. But the monk was not entirely stable, either. There was a profound conflict inside him. But he controlled himself and said: "Well, you should not have come here; come to my hut after a couple of days. This place is for lonely yogis, and you should not stay here any longer."[31]

In spite of its author's deliberate desire to write a good contemporary piece as an answer to Prem Chand's objection, or perhaps because of it, *The Skeleton* is rather heavy handed. The poetic quality of his language, so helpful to him in rendering intense dramatic conflicts and emotions in his short stories and plays, hinders the development of this patently problem-oriented novel. The characters are less than half real and the plot is burdened with too many subsidiary details. Although the sordid details of moral corruption and promiscuousness underline the decadence of the society Prasad set out to satirize, the novel lacks credibility and its social realism is overshadowed by a deus-ex-machina manipulation of events. The various subplots are joined together by forces that are alien to the novel in the sense that they are never justified.

Some Hindi critics, unwilling to accept that the author of *Kamayani* could have failed at anything, overestimate *The Skeleton*, but most are, admittedly with some reluctance, willing to grant that it is not a successful work, even for a first novel. Pandey's opinion is typical: "There is a kind of heaviness about it, a certain lack of structure. One must not forget that Prasad was primarily a poet, and his works are predominantly emotional and poetic. *Kankal* is no exception. It is full of poetic passages embodying progressive ideas. Their presence indicates a poetic genius, and we are impressed by it. But someone keeps insisting: 'Wish *Kankal* were a poem.' "[32] Pandey puts his criticism of *The Skeleton* in the mildest possible terms, but, it is obvious, that even he cannot gloss over the fact that this is not a successful work.

The main reason for the failure of *The Skeleton* is its lack of irony. Prasad takes Prem Chand's objection with utter seriousness, but fails to translate it with the kind of detachment and irony he shows in *One Sip*. What could have been a successful social satire turns into a pamphlet, the parts of which do not quite hang together.

Having tried his hand at the short story, with some remarkable successes to his credit, and the novel with little success, Prasad returns to drama, the form he had almost perfected in *Skandgupta*. The return to drama is accompanied by a return to the glorious past of India, a period Prasad felt immensely comfortable with. He preferred to examine the question "Where are we?" through "Where do we come from?" and seek an explanation of the present rather than merely describe it. He has sometimes been accused of escaping into the past, and the criticism is at least partially justified. But, as he pointed out himself, his interest in the past was motivated by a search for an explanation of the present and a desire to vindicate the forgotten aspects of Indian tradition. His concern with the past and what he construed to be the real Indian tradition is taken up again in his next dramatic masterpiece, *Chandragupta*.

Chapter Five

The Return to Drama

Chandragupta

As early as 1909, Prasad had published a research essay on Chandragupta, the well-known Indian king.[1] Chandragupta fascinated him and, according to Gupta, he always wanted to write a play about him.[2] The 1912 experiment, *The Wedding of Kalyani* [*Kalyani Parinay*], did not quite satisfy him. His dissatisfaction with D. L. Roy's *Chandragupta*, the Hindi translation of which appeared in 1917, must have further prompted him to take up his favorite subject once more. Although submitted to the press, according to Gupta, as early as 1928, it came out only in 1931.[3]

Generally considered to be his best play, *Chandragupta* is about India at the time of Alexander's invasion. The major incidents that make up *Chandragupta* are historically verifiable. The playwright has added or subtracted very little, merely filling in the colors, as Manav has correctly pointed out, within the framework provided by history.[4] The internally divided India at the time of Alexander's invasion provides the historical background for *Chandragupta*.[5] The internal rivalries of India make the invader's task easier. Poros ends up fighting him alone because Ambhik, the King of Gandhar, and Nand, the King of Magadh, refuse to help.[6]

The play opens at Taxila, where Chanakya, the legendary author of *Arthashastra*, and the prince of Magadha are discussing matters of state.[7] Ambhik arrives and picks a fight with the prince. He threatens to kill him, but is stopped by Chandragupta, an early indication of the role of Chandragupta throughout the play.

Chandragupta, seconded by Chanakya, requests Nand's help for Poros but he declines. Poros had turned Nand's daughter down and Nand sees it as his chance to get even with him.[8] Chanakya does not approve of Nand's petty thinking, and tells him so. Nand orders his arrest. He is, however, later helped out of prison by Chandragupta. Chanakya tries to get some help for Poros from Ambhik, but, once again, is turned down. Chandragupta soon meets Alexander, who asks for help in attacking Magadh. Chandragupta, of course, declines, and escapes being taken prisoner. A series of complicated battles and counterbattles leads to Chandragupta's becoming commander-in-chief, and later replacing Nand, the king. He marries Cornellia, the daughter of Seleucid.[9]

Most of the attacks and counterattacks, intrigues and their resolutions, are planned and controlled by the master strategist, Chanakya, who, in many ways, is really far more impressive and powerful than Chandragupta, who at times seems a mere pawn in the hands of the chessmaster. Chandragupta himself accuses Chanakya of controlling just a bit too much: "Why are you enjoying this endless privilege? You not only want to control the affairs of the empire but also the personal affairs of my family."[10]

Chanakya's response, contained in perhaps one of the most memorable utterances of *Chandragupta*, is extremely revealing and brutally disarming:

I never wanted to run the empire, Chandragupta. I am a Brahman: Feeling was my empire and Love my religion. I was at peace—a loving inhabitant of the Kingdom of Bliss. The Sun, the Moon and the Stars were my sources of life, the Sky my cover, the Earth my bed, intellectual amusement my work, and satisfaction my capital. And look how far away I am from my natural habitat. Intrigue in place of cooperation, thorns in place of flowers, fear in place of love, cunning in place of knowledge! Take away your right, Chandragupta! That will be my rebirth. The political intrigues have left permanent scars in my soul. I am running after a mirage. I have lost my peace, can't even recognize myself.[11]

And that from the Indian Machiavelli! Sounds more like the tragic confessions of an overreacher!

What are Chanakya's motives? There are those who say that he is guided only by revenge, a sort of motiveless malignity. But he seems to be too sensitive to be a Iago. He wants the traditional role of the Brahman, to counsel, restored, and, as he sees it, it is incumbent upon him to end factionalism and help fight off the alien threat represented by Alexander. One of his earliest pieces of advice to his princely pupils is to stand up not for their own little kingdoms but for India: "You are the prince of Malav, and he the prince of Magadh. Is that the limit of your pride? In order to keep your pride, you will have to forget Malav and Magadh and concentrate on India. Can't you see that our little kingdoms will all be soon taken over by alien rulers."[12]

Chandragupta seems to be the most capable man, and Chanakya, according to Manav, does not use his sharp intellect and impressive power for any personal purpose but only for the public good, the Brahmanic ideal of Chanakya. Very early in the play, he tells the prince of Taxila: "My dear prince, a Brahman does not depend on any one nor is he the subject of anyone. He lives in his own kingdom as if he were an immortal. Don't be too proud of your rank. A Brahman, though he has the power to obtain everything, rejects your material rewards."[13]

He cannot, however, suffer fools easily, and is inclined to interpret institutional rejection as personal affront. He cannot stand petty princes and cowardly kings who dare ignore the importance of the role of a Brahman such as he. He takes as much interest in restoring the integrity of the empire as in destroying, with a vengeance, the house of Nand. When Nand orders him dragged out of his court, he tells the king what he plans to do: "Sure, you can have me dragged out! You are, after all, a dog brought up on the leftovers of an untouchable! The hair that is being pulled now will turn into serpents that will poison the Nands."[14]

The extent to which the noble soul of even Chanakya is corrupted, for he too is caught in the political trap, is an indication

The Return to Drama

of the moral decline of the universe around him. He comes out, but not without deep scars. The pursuit of knowledge is possible without such scars, but knowledge, when transformed into wisdom, inevitably loses some of its purity. The loss of that purity is the price Chanakya has to pay for attempting to take an active role in the utilization of his immense knowledge of men and morals. He gives the world of *Chandragupta* far more than he takes from it, but the world he sets out to change has to crucify him. To solve human problems, one needs a human motive. Chanakya lets revenge be his. He cannot control his joy in showing up a fool. The scars in his soul are left not by his dream of an integrated India but by the personal delight he has taken in eliminating the petty little pebbles that made it difficult for him to walk, as a Brahman is supposed to, barefoot.

Chanakya's conflict makes him very human, and he is clearly one of the most remarkable characters in Modern Hindi literature. Although Prasad was considerably helped by a wealth of facts and legends about Chanakya, the Chanakya of *Chandragupta* has a personality of his own. Here is Chanakya begging, in his inimitable style, Nand to help Poros fight the alien invader:

Nand: "Who are you that speak without authority?"
Chanakya: "A Brahman graduate of Taxila."
Nand: "Brahman, Brahman! The fires of their power are burning everywhere."
Chanakya: "Not anymore, your lordship. There's no more fire. Only a few sparks are left."
Rakhas: "Even then, there's that much heat."
Chanakya: "That's inevitable. When even that disappears, India will too. If you are thinking of eliminating them, do give up the idea. Only Brahmans can take care of the welfare of the nation. Buddha, who is afraid of violence, could not possibly take care of the troubles around us."
Nand: "Brahman! If you don't know how to talk, learn to be quiet."

Chanakya: "That's what I went to learn at Taxila, your lordship. I not only learnt there, but also taught there. I cannot therefore accept that I am a fool."[15]

Although Chandragupta sometimes, and only sometimes, appears to be merely an instrument of Chanakya's policies, he is able to hold his own. "It is satisfying to note," observes Manav, "that Prasad is not content to let Chandragupta be only a puppet in the hands of Chanakya. The play *Mudrarakshas* [a sixth-century Sanskrit play about Chanakya by Vishakha Datta] has this as its major weakness. Chanakya and Chandragupta are complementary to each other. Chanakya is the brain, and Chandragupta the muscle. Both are needed for the establishment of the empire."[16] After all, it is Chandragupta that asks Chanakya for an explanation.

Even the minor characters of *Chandragupta* are alive. The proud Poros, the pompous Nand, the docile Cornellia, and even the unknown students of Taxila are all skillfully portrayed. Although the stage is dominated by Chanakya, the other actors can hold their own and manage to leave a lasting impression. They all speak in authentic voices:

Ambhik: "What explosion? Young man, who are you?"
Sinharan: "A citizen of Malava."
Ambhik: "No, you have to be more specific."
Sinharan: "A Taxila student."[17]

The dialogue of *Chandragupta* is refreshingly bidirectional: both interlocuters participate as they are supposed to. Here is a randomly chosen example:

Parvateshvara: "Beautiful Alka, how long will you be here?"
Alka: "That depends on him who has taken me a prisoner."
Parvateshvara: "Who can do that? That's unfair, Alka. Come, the palace is waiting for you."
Alka: "No, Paurav. I'm scared of palaces because they imprison your mind for ever."[18]

The language of *Chandragupta* is not only genuinely bidirectional but also sharp and crisp:

Nand: "Be quiet."
Chanakya: "After one more statement, your lordship."
Rakhasas: "What?"
Chanakya: "The foreigners are making inroads. . . . Magadh should help Parvateshvara."[19]

Chandragupta is tightly structured and presents a forceful dramatization of the petty rivalries that made India an easy prey to foreign invaders and rulers. It is a frankly nationalistic play, but the nationalism is not expressed in rhetorical attacks against alien forces. The alien invader is only an outsider. The problem is an internal one. While Chanakya's speeches emphasize the need for internal cooperation, its numerous nationalistic lyrics celebrate the strength and potential that have always been there:

> Brave and immortal, make up your mind
> The path is right, march on, march on
>
> > Innumerable rays
> > Blaze like a fire;
> > Beloved of the mother-land
> > Don't stop ever!
>
> Non-stop swim through the sea of battle
> Be brave and victorious, march on, march on.[20]

Chandragupta underlines Prasad's dramatic objectivity. The Prasad that so sympathetically portrays the Buddhist doctrine of love in *Ajatshatru* does not refrain from adopting the opposite point of view and attacking Buddhism for its inaction. The conflict between action and introspection is not a metaphysical problem that can be solved once for all. Each age must resolve it anew and the age of Chandragupta clearly called for a reactivation of the wheel of action. Chanakya sets it in motion and prevents the complete subjugation of a nation. Although Prasad, unlike Prem Chand and Gandhi, was not a man of action himself, *Chandragupta* clearly shows that he not only appreciated such men but also the sheer necessity of having them appear when circumstances warrant action rather than meditation.

Dhruvaswamini

The dramatic style inaugurated with *Vishakha* is concluded with *Dhruvaswamini*, published in 1933. An extremely powerful, and in many ways original, play, *Dhruvaswamini* deals with the place of women in Indian society. It is a serious effort to show that the return to the past was in fact motivated by a desire to find constructs that could help understand the present and rid the society of many taboos that have no traditional sanction. Prasad takes pains to argue in the preface to the play that Dhruvaswamini's revolt against her impotent and decadent husband, Ramgupta, had all the backing of tradition.[21]

While on a pleasure trip to central India, Ramgupta is attacked by Shakraj, who demands Dhruvaswamini in exhange for a compromise. Ramgupta is willing to trade her off, but Chandragupta arrives on the scene in time to save Dhruvaswamini from either being traded or killing herself. In order to teach Shakraj a lesson, Chandragupta, disguised as Dhruvaswamini, smuggles himself into his camp. Shakraj is killed, and Chandragupta takes over his fort. Ramgupta arrives and imprisons Chandragupta, but not for long. Ramgupta's marriage is declared void by the priests, and Chandragupta becomes the official ruler of Magadha.

Dhruvaswamini has a straightforward plot, and, like *Skandgupta*, an extremely well-defined focus. There are only two songs in the play and its dialogue is terse and pointed. An exquisitely structured short play, it is a true masterpiece. It is also the first Hindi play in which a woman stands up to fight for her traditionally defined rights. She is not a feminist, and is perfectly willing to accept her role as the wife of a man she does not love, but

The Return to Drama

when he refuses to accept her traditional rights, she does not hesitate in challenging him.

A dramatic justification for remarriage constructed out of the pages of ancient Indian history, *Dhruvaswamini* is perhaps one of Prasad's most radical plays. That this radical solution is forged out of the conflict between traditional roles is indicative of Prasad's profound concern for the time honored conventions that define Indian civilization. The preface notes: "It is true that our holy books are not always clear about practical issues. We are, however, just a bit too anxious to call modern reforms and sociological experiments un-Indian, but I am certain that ancient India, with its long tradition, tried almost every system of values."[22] The purpose of *Dhruvaswamini* is to retrieve one of those systems of values and to put the stamp of traditional sanction on it. Many such experiments have apparently been lost to history, and when tried anew are assumed to be un-Indian.

Prasad has sometimes been accused of being too much of a traditionalist. *Dhruvaswamini*, however, demonstrates that his love of tradition was neither superficial nor ritualistic. He was a conservative in the best sense of the word. Although womanhood, faith, and forgiveness are synonymous terms in his works, the queen of Magadha leaves no doubt that his doll's house was perfectly capable of accommodating a Nora.

The virtues of tradition have to be respected by all sides. A Brahman is expected to regard personal satisfaction as his wages, and the king is expected to listen to his wise counsel. The king's refusal to play his role leads the former to do what he thought was best. The queen is expected to operate under certain constraints, but the king is expected to protect her. She pleads to her husband to protect her honor and asks him: "Is my womanhood not entitled to even that from a man who considers himself to be my lord?"[23] But he is too afraid of his own life, forcing her to take the role of an assertive, independent woman. "I am not only a queen," she says, "but also a woman."[24] But when he does not keep his part of the bargain she walks off.

The impact of Dhruvaswamini's revolt is intensely dramatic precisely because she is not seeking independence for its own sake, but has it thrust upon her by the inability of the system that assigned her the secondary role to keep its side of the bargain. She is willing to sacrifice her individuality, but not her integrity; after all, the tradition that taught her to be a good, obedient queen also taught her to expect certain things from the king. She loved Chandragupta but offered to be the king's wife; but, when the king ignores her traditionally defined rights, she rises to meet the challenge. When the protector of the doll's castle refuses to play his role, the doll becomes a woman: "I just want to say that I cannot be subjected to the male practice of treating women as inanimate property. If you cannot protect me and if you cannot protect the prestige of your family, then you cannot sell me either. I will leave myself to save you from any trouble."[25]

The problem of *Dhruvaswamini* is clearly defined and the conflicts it generates both for the protagonist and others are sharply dramatized. "As far as effectiveness, simplicity, and intensity of conflict are concerned," Bahuguna argues, "*Dhruvaswamini* is perhaps the best of Prasad's plays."[26] The simplicity of its plot gives it a sharpness of focus not seen even in *Skandgupta*.

Chapter Six

The Lyric and the Novel Revisited

Emotions Recollected in Tranquillity

His dramatic output alone would have established Prasad as a major Hindi writer, but, apparently, he was not content with his success with drama only. He had originally started out as a lyrical poet and the lyrical strain is constantly present in his work. His success with drama, however, gave him what he needed to enrich his lyrical poetry. The first proof of the benefits is to be found in his revised version of *Tears*.

Composed during 1923–24, *Tears*, perhaps his most popular work, was first published in 1925. Its second, revised edition came out in 1933. The first edition is a somewhat loosely structured collection of 126 stanzas of two lines each. The second edition, however, contains 190 rather closely knit stanzas.

The changes that Prasad made in revising the first edition are very significant, both linguistically and thematically. The first edition seems to express emotions as felt; the second, emotions recalled in tranquillity. While the first edition generates pity and pathos, the second inspires a genuinely tragic response. The first edition is dominated by the "I fall upon the thorns of life, I bleed" syndrome of a young romantic; the second reorganizes this feverish and self-pitying outburst into a controlled reflection on the nature and place of sorrow in human life.

The eight years intervening between the first and second editions give Prasad the necessary distance that makes the 1933 edition something more than a mere register of personal grievances. The time-depth helps Prasad turn the first edition into a philosophical, semimystical, long lyric about the significance and ultimate meaning of personal sorrow. The second edition becomes a dramatized discussion of sorrow.

Distancing and dramatization are, in fact, the major effects of changes made. Its stanzas are organized to provide something of a narrative framework to its lyrical expressions. This brings structure. Distancing is accomplished by extremely simple, yet effective, linguistic devices—the present tense is replaced by the past, the second-person pronoun by its third-person counterpart, and proximal pronouns by distant pronouns. The immediate proximity of reminders of pain acquires a distance and is now filtered through memory to be expressed as *there* and not *here*.

A few examples will be sufficient to show the remarkable distancing achieved by these simple linguistic devices. For: "What sorrow did I cause you/Which made taking pleasure away necessary." we find: "What sorrow did I cause her/Which made taking pleasure necessary."[1] And for what appears to be a description of an impending disaster in the first edition: "The storm is raging/And the lightning is dangerous" we find a much less threatening flashback in the second edition: "The storm was raging/And the lightning dangerous."[2] Actually the change to the past tense makes the newer version more "modal" in the sense that it can be interpreted as "The storm seemed raging, and the lightning dangerous."

There are other changes too, indicative of Prasad's growing command of the language. In the second edition he simplifies, for example, quite a few consonant clusters and removes some reduplicated forms. All these changes taken together make *Tears* an exquisite long lyrical narrative, and establish the unmistakable appearance of a major poetic voice. The motivation for these changes, and the care taken in executing them, confirm Shah's assertion that Prasad is primarily an intellectual poet.[3]

Tears begins by asking the question, "Why does the heart feel

The Lyric and the Novel Revisited

so full of sorrow?" and offering the answer that the memory of the great union, which had been repressed for so long, is anxious to express itself now.[4] The description of personal sorrow is, however, more often than not achieved in terms that are impersonal. The images that are utilized to express the sense of personal loneliness are drawn from the elemental forces of nature. They underline the intensity and create a universe larger than the narrator's private world.

The narrator goes on to describe the beauty of the beloved in terms that are now hackneyed, now novel, but always sensuous:

> Covering your moon-like face with a veil
> And hiding the lamp with the sari
> In the twilight of my life
> As a surprise you came.[5]

The comparison between the moon and the beloved's face is as old as Indian literature, but the last two lines of the stanza are the marks of an unfamiliar voice.

The combination of the old and the new is, in fact, one of the most striking features of the imagery of *Tears*. But what is even more impressive is the recombination of old images. There is, for example, nothing new about "black eyes," "the red of youth," "red wine," and "the wine glass," but the restructuring achieved in the following stanza is really refreshing:

> How much do these black eyes
> Contain the red of youth?
> Ruby wine has been poured
> Into this jade glass by whom?[6]

There is nothing new about the moonlike face of the beloved or serpentlike hair (the latter is at least as old as Jayasi[7]), but the following stanza plays with the old images in a refreshingly new way:

> Who tied the Moon
> With these black chains?
> Why the fangs of these snakes
> Are full of diamonds?[8]

Having indulged in self-pity and having relished the old images that come back to mind with erotic intensity, the narrator soon puts his personal sorrow into a larger framework: "This smile and that fear, let them mix together/Let it rain again, and let new buds blossom."[9] He hopes that his personal sorrow will bring new enlightenment into this world. He concludes by likening his fears to morning dew:

> Distill the essence of all
> And in the driest of lives
> Rain like the morning dew
> Covering the globe with your grace![10]

Perhaps the most impressive thing about *Tears* is its essentially dual structure. Each stanza is a self-contained unit, rather like a *rubai*[11] expressing a full thought that has its own beginning, middle, and end, and yet all 190 of them are arranged in an easily perceptible narrative sequence. "*Ansoo*," says Bajpai, "is a necklace of pearls in which each pearl is exquisitely cut and is, at the same time, a unit in the necklace."[12]

This duality of structure also operates at the thematic level. While the first edition of *Tears* seems to be concerned exclusively with the theme of personal sorrow, generated by separation from a human beloved, the second edition, because of the changes discussed above, acquires an additional dimension that not only allows and encourages but almost forces the reader to interpret it simultaneously as an account of separation from a human beloved and from God.

The terminology of affectionate respect, when expressing a profoundly felt sense of deep gratitude, quite naturally approximates the terminology of worship, and the intensified, slightly hyper-

The Lyric and the Novel Revisited

bolic, expressions of personal encounters easily assume a superhuman dimension:

> Proud was I that you came down
> My beloved to meet me
> Swept off my feet, I was surprised
> Much as awakened by a morning dream.[13]

The essentially elemental and grand quality of the recurrent images of *Tears*—the sky, the moon, the ocean—not only effectively captures the magnitude of the separation at the human level, but also easily provides it with the timeless props of a cosmic stage:

> The bubbles of the ocean broke
> So did the garland of stars
> And the skyless earth
> Seemed to have been taken.[14]

The question, sometimes raised by native Hindi critics, as to which of these levels of interpretation is the intended one seems almost irrelevant. The language and the structure of *Tears* seem to require a double interpretation.

The maturity responsible for the revised version of *Tears* can also be seen in *The Wave* [*Lahar*], a collection of lyrics also published in 1933. Most of the lyrics of *The Wave* are devoted to traditional romantic subjects of love, nature, hope, and despair. The lyrical intensity of *The Wave*, however, is mellow, for the artist is in better control of his materials. The most autobiographical and personal of these lyrics concludes with a refusal to indulge in self-pity: "Isn't it better that I listen to others and be quiet/Why do you want to hear the story of my life anyway?/Moreover, it is not time yet."[15]

While the narrator of *Tears* is only too eager to give vent to his sorrows and disappointments, the lyrical voices of *The Wave* are almost critical of that attitude: "Why do you scream/That you were never loved?"[16]

Even when attention is turned to the more memorable past, the main concern of *Tears*, the emphasis is on a quiet reflection on the beauty of those days and not on the contemporary sadness.

The lyricist of *The Wave* is interested in waves, stars, and sunsets for their own sake and not because they provide a ready-made stage for his pathetic fallacies. Here is an example that describes the movement of a wave:

> Rise, rise, little wave, roll, rise
> Like the yawn of compassion
> And the shadow of ocean breeze
> On this dry shore to break and sprinkle.[17]

In *The Wave*, it is nature that seems to determine the feelings of the lyricist rather than the other way around. He is perfectly willing to celebrate the beauty of things around him. He looks at them through his own eyes, but makes no effort to filter his perceptions through his personal sorrows. Here are the opening lines of a lyric devoted to celebrating the beauty of the predawn sky: "In the chambers of the horizon, Dawn still sleeps/And the East End Bar is not yet open."[18] The search for calm and certitude and peace that pass the personal grievances characterizes what is perhaps the best-known lyric from *The Wave*:

> Take me, take me there
> My sailor, slowly, slowly
> Where the ocean wave
> Deep in the ears of the sky
> Tells an innocent love story.[19]

The lyrics of *The Wave* are clearly romantic in nature, but they represent romanticism at its best. They exhibit the kind of dramatic control one normally associates with poems like Keats's "Ode on a Grecian Urn," passionate but well wrought, intense but unsentimental.

The language of *The Wave* is polished and appropriate for the quiet, reflective mood of its lyrics. The soft quietness of the mood is captured by a diction remarkably consistent in its phonological structure. The lyric describing the slow arrival of the dawn, for example, contains fifty-six words, but only two with consonantal clusters, and even there the first member of the cluster is a sonorant nasal, a sound type closer to vowels in its musicality than it is to other consonants. Consonantal clusters are as a matter of fact very rare in *The Wave*. The high density of vowels and vowellike consonants is, quite obviously, not random. It is a result of careful and systematic stylistic choices made by the lyricist. The lyrics of *The Wave* are exceptionally musical. They are "waves of melody" that "sing themselves almost automatically upon the reader's tongue."[20]

A few of the poems in *The Wave* deal with history. One of them is devoted to Ashoka's sadness after the Kalinga campaign. It shows Ashoka, the great warrior, sad at the destruction caused by him:

> The Earth doth burn, the mountains kindle
> And woeful is the universe entire
> And thorns at every step do greet our feet
> And this pathetic route of burning sand![21]

Poems like "Ashoka's Worry" and "The Shadow of Destruction" ["Pralaya Ki Chhaya"] are dramatic monologues that can easily compare, according to Sahney, with "the best specimens of their kind in Browning."[22]

The Wave is Prasad's last collection of lyrics. The lyrical intensity of *Tears* and the Keatsian control of *The Wave* are subjected to a more severe test within the epic framework of *Kamayani*.

Another Try at the Novel

The Wave was followed by a light romantic novel, *Titali* (1934). Although better constructed than *The Skeleton*, it is essentially a slight work.[23] It is the story of a young girl, Titali, who falls in love with and marries the somewhat impassionate Madhua. Circumstances engulf Madhua in a series of misfortunes and crimes, and he is forced to run away to Calcutta. Titali is forced to wait for him till her son is fourteen. Having survived a maze of complications that include a murder, Madhua comes back. The story is, however, punctuated heavily by the events in the lives of many people around Titali, particularly those in the life of Indradeva, the local landlord, and his English friend Shaila, the daughter of an English woman who used to live in India at the height of the British empire.

The novel attempts to capture both the spirit of the healthy innocent romance between Madhua and Titali and the nature of cross-cultural confrontation that ensues when Indradeva brings an alien into the midst of a feudalistic social structure. It also seeks to provide a critical commentary on the greed of the local bureaucrats employed by the landed aristocracy during the British Raj in India. The tone of the book is, however, generally mild, and even when subjects severely attacked in *The Skeleton* are approached, one finds the criticisms less than biting.

Though full of pathos and incidents approaching the tragic, the novel ends on a happy note. The happy ending, however, seems to be the result of a heavy-handed use of the oldest of Indian gods and goddesses: Fate. The sequence of events is almost as bizarre as that in *The Skeleton* and there is about as much justification for it as in the earlier novel. Kamlesh observes: "The birth of Titali, her childhood, her youth, and her maturity are all handled by Fate: from London to Banaras! An English woman with an Indian name!! And, at the end, everybody reunites."[24]

The all-pervasive use of Fate has sometimes been attributed to his philosophy of determinism, but very often no such philosophical interpretation is possible. Some of his plays are as fatalistic as *The Skeleton* or *Titali*, but the events in them seem justified. Determinism and fatalism as philosophical postures do not constitute an explanation for a haphazard collection of unmotivated actions and unjustifiable events. It is one thing to be philosophically concerned with the problem of determinism and quite another to use it as an excuse for artistic failure. The former leads to a heightened awareness of the role played by circumstances beyond our control; the latter, only to second-rate literature. *Titali* and *The Skeleton* do not deepen or heighten our awareness of forces beyond our perceptual threshold, they merely beg us to let things go for the sake of convenience.

Although not entirely a satisfactory work, *Titali* does represent an advance over *The Skeleton*. Prasad takes a smaller piece of the universe in *Titali*, and he employs a more realistic language to describe it. Although he never quite abandons his love of purple passages, so abundant in *The Skeleton*, the syntax of *Titali* is far less cumbersome than the syntax of *The Skeleton*. The characters use a language that suits them rather than employ an artificial High Hindi that is not quite apppropriate to their rather mundane concerns.

The cultural conflict resulting from the relationship between Indradeva and Shaila, though not the main concern of the novel, is sensitively described. The suspicion Shaila is subjected to and the reluctance with which she is accepted by her peers are very carefully handled.

Although better than *The Skeleton, Titali* remains a second-rate novel. This return to mundane social problems of daily life from the imaginative world of *Tears* and *The Wave* proves once more that Prasad could not handle the hard rocks of contemporary social problems, Prem Chand's specialty.

Chapter Seven

The Epic Voice: *Kamayani*

Introduction

Kavya means "poetry" and *maha* means "great." The compound noun *mahakavya,* however, means "epic." Not all epics contain great poetry, but the definitional interchangeability is an understandable temptation for Hindi poets. Poets who write great poetry, as Prasad obviously did, are, at least within the tradition he was a part of, expected to write an epic as their final test. Prasad accepted the traditional challenge and the result was *Kamayani.*

Composed during a period of eight years, *Kamayani,* unquestionably the most important achievement of Modern Hindi, was first published in 1937. Prasad started work on it as early as 1925 and everything he did between 1925 and 1936 can be legitimately regarded as a preparation for his masterpiece. The development of Prasad from his first major work, *Tears,* to *Dhruvaswamini* leads directly to *Kamayani.*

Kamayani represents the final culmination of Prasad's literary experimentation.[1] Even his critics find that it is not easy to belittle the epic proportions and depth of *Kamayani*! *Kamayani* is the final product of a successful lyricist, playwright, novelist, and critic, and, as such, it is a remarkable blend of lyrical intensity, dramatic distance, narrative control, and critical acumen.

The Narrative: A Brief Summary

Its epic dimensions can be gathered even from its threadbare

The Epic Voice: Kamayani

narrative. It revolves around Manu. At the beginning of the epic, he finds himself alone atop a lofty mountain peak, surrounded by doom and destruction. Worried and disturbed, he tries hard to come to terms with past memories and future prospects. The waters of doom, however, soon recede and Shradha, who later offers to become his companion, arrives on the scene bringing some hope to the shattered kingdom of gloom. The ray of hope soon transforms itself into a rainbow of desire: Manu encounters Kama, the Indian god of love, in a dream sequence and the guest and the host become one. Shradha has doubts about what she has done but is reassured by her mother. Manu, however, becomes selfish and leaves Shradha when he finds out that she is pregnant. He ventures into the Kingdom of Sarasvat, where he meets Ida. He runs the affairs of of her state and brings some order into it. He threatens the scheme of things, however, by attempting to seduce Ida. His transgression activates a rebellion and he is knocked unconscious. When he regains consciousness, he finds Shradha and their son there. He apologizes profusely but, burdened with guilt, leaves again. Shradha sets out to find him again. She does, and the epic ends with their son joining them.

Kamayani: Detailed Outline

Divided into fifteen cantos, *Kamayani* opens with a dramatic announcement of its protagonist's plight after the great deluge:

> On the lofty peak of the Himalayas,
> Under the icy shade of a rock,
> A man was sitting with moist eyes,
> Watching the rolling waters of doom![2]

The task Prasad sets for himself is nothing less than the reconstruction of a world, justifying the powers the first cousins of Manu would have assumed a poet had. *Kamayani* is, thus, a world constructed with words, and Prasad puts all that he ever learned into it. The earlier conflicts, the later resolutions, and the sign posts en route all find a proper place within the encompassing framework of *Kamayani*.

The first canto, entitled "Anxiety" ["Chinta"], describes the lonely Manu watching, from a mountain peak, the devastating deluge around him:

> High above was frozen snow,
> While surging waters rolled below,
> One primal energy pervades in them,
> Matter or life, whatever the name.[3]

and "mourning over the dead glories of gods" while "On the turbulent ocean down-below/Waves were dashed to poignant death."[4]

He is helped out of his despair by the disappearance of the rising vapor around him and the arrival of a golden dawn, the description of which opens the second canto, "Hope" ["Asha"]:

> Usha dawned like the victorious Lakshmi
> Showering golden arrows all around;
> The defeated night of doom retreated
> And sank in the recesses of the deep
>
> The anemic face of terrorized Nature
> Started smiling again today;
> Rains having ended, creation commenced
> Unfolding its natural growth anew.[5]

On seeing "the drowsy shrubs awake to wash their faces in refreshing water," Manu becomes full of strength and vigor, "like the radiant sun glowing in mid-horizon"[6] and hopes to find someone to share his joy with.

The arrival of Shradha, described in the next canto, fulfills his hope.[7] On seeing her, Manu is at a loss for words:

> What should I say, am I so deluded
> Under this canopy of the azure heaven,

The Epic Voice: Kamayani

> Like a stranded wave or gusty breeze
> In the shattered Kingdom of a gloomy void?
> Like an unconscious *stupa*[8] of forgetfulness,
> Like a blurred reflection of hazy light,
> Or like the existence of insentient life,
> Victory is shrouded in collective delay.[9]

He, however, soon finds some words to say to Shradha, who offers to become his companion.

The third canto: "Desire" ["Kama"], is devoted to a dream sequence in which Kama, the mythic god of love, introduces himself to Manu: by describing the role he and his wife, Rati, played in the lives of gods and goddesses of the by-gone era:[10]

> I would enkindle desire in them,
> Should slake their amorous thirst.
> Ecstatic joys were blended in harmony
> As we led them on their destined path.[11]

and exhorts Manu to become worthy of Shradha in order to win her affection.

The fully expected reunion between the guest and the host forms the subject matter of the next canto, "Passion" ["Vasana"]. Manu approaches her with love and she,

> Like a smoky creeper that doesn't twine,
> Around the tree of sky,
> But becomes laden in the wintry night
> By a new burden of dew drops.[12]

stoops under the weight of youth, her voice choked with emotion.

The fifth cano, "Bashfulness" ["Lajja"], describes the internal conflict generated in Shradha by her submission to Manu. Shradha has doubts about what she has done, but Rati, her mother, assures her:

> Woman! you are an abiding Faith
> Trust, is silvery Himalayan Vales,

> Like an ambrosial stream you flow
> Over the beautiful plains of life.[13]

Manu's old self returns soon after Shradha's submission to her. Kilat and Akuli help bring the old Manu out in "Action" ["Karma"]. The Manu that had blamed his ancestors for the disaster from which he is trying to recover now muses:

> How very charming are lovely links,
> Of those ancestral traditional Karmas[14]
> In which are entangled those happy hours
> Ever fulfilling our desires of life![15]

Manu becomes selfish and resists Shradha's suggestion that he should be a little less selfish. The differences are, however, resolved later and they end up in each others' arms;

> In between those wooden sticks,
> In that solitary cozy cave,
> Fiery flame quietly quelled down
> Like the happy dreams on waking.[16]

Manu's selfishness, the theme of the next canto, "Envy" ["Irshya"], surfaces again when he finds out that Shradha is pregnant and unable to give him as much attention as he would like. He calls Shradha's unwillingness "A mere device for dividing affection"[17] and, unable to accept just his share, announces: "I depart right now, just leaving behind,/The filled up burden of pent-up emotions./I shall gladly welcome the pricking thorns."[18] He leaves a tired Shradha alone, calling impatiently: "Stop, listen, Oh! heartless one."[19]

Manu ventures into Sarasvat, a kingdom ready to fall apart. The queen of Sarasvat, Ida, for whom the sixth canto is named is looking for someone who can conduct the affairs of her state and bring some order into it.[20] Manu takes over the role, convinced

The Epic Voice: Kamayani

that he has found what he wants: "Let the entire life be a call for action,/Let the gates of prosperity and joy be unlocked."[21]

A summary of events to follow is presented in the form of a dream dreamt by Shradha in the next canto, appropriately called "Dream" ["Swapna"]. Manu's efforts to seduce Ida produce a revolt, both in nature and in his people:

> Nature was terribly oppressed all around
> Shiva lifted his foot in the *Tandav*[22] dance.
> Entire creation and all the living beings,
> Were becoming as if akin to a dream.
> All were impatiently seeking shelter,
> While Manu was yet sceptic about his sin,
> Earth was trembling terribly frightened,
> Again apprehending a dreadful disaster.[23]

"Struggle" ["Sangharsh"], the canto that follows, portrays the reality underlying the dream described in the previous canto. Manu's attempt to seduce Ida does, in fact, create a rebellion. Ida tries to convince Manu that he is transgressing, but he refuses to listen to her "timely" warning that "If law-makers don't abide/By the laws exact/Then certainly all shall perish."[24] He, in his selfishness, threatens to construct a separate world "Full of shrieks and wails."[25] And he actually does. The price he has to pay, however, is rather heavy: he is knocked unconscious, "While the earth was drenched,/By the river of blood in spate."[26]

When Manu regains consciousness, he finds Shradha and their son there. His profuse apologies and repentance are what the next canto, "Renunciation" ["Nirveda"] is devoted to. Unable to face Shradha, he, "with a tarnished face and sinful body,"[27] decides to leave his wife and son again so that "When they woke up in the early morn,/They saw that Manu was not there."[28]

Manu's son is confused, and the burden of explanation falls on Shradha who tries to cope with it in the antepenultimate canto, "Revelation" ["Darshan"]. Shradha, in spite of Manu's betrayal, offers an essentially optimistic explanation to her son, utterly confused by the events around him: "In its every layer lies implicit peace,/So deeply refreshing, sorrow is delusion."[29]

Ida is also impressed by Shradha's generosity and apologizes for her selfishness. Shradha points out to Ida that she has looked at the world from a somewhat restricted perspective, a perspective that ignores emotions and feelings. She offers her son to help Ida to attempt to construct another world in which emotion and reason are blended in harmony. She herself, however, sets out to rediscover Manu. She finds him and he, begging forgiveness once again, asks her to lead him:

> What's this? Shradha! oh! Do lead me!
> To those Divine Feet, oh! give me support
> In which all good and evil are smelted
> To become pure and very smoothing.[30]

In the penultimate canto, "Secret"["Rahasya"], Shradha assumes the role of the explicator once again as they go on their ultimate mythological voyage and as she points out the triangle of Desire, Action, and Knowledge to Manu. She explains to Manu the important fact that he is the central point of that triangle. The triangle he beholds, she explains to him, presents one of the most devastating paradoxes of life, for:

> Bereft of knowledge, opposed to action,
> Then how can cherished desires be fulfilled?
> This is the bewildering irony of their life.
> Knowledge and action are opposed to Truth.[31]

The paradox is, however, resolved as

> Like a ray of glorious light,
> The smile of Shradha ran through them.
> Suddenly they all were linked together,
> While the blazing fire glowed in them.[32]

The last canto, "Bliss" ["Anand"], brings Ida and Shradha's son also to the spot where Shradha and Manu had observed the synthesis of Desire, Action, and Knowledge. The epic ends as all differences are obliterated:

> Matter and spirit were harmonious
> Exquisite was the form of Beauty
> Consciousness alone was blossoming
> Transcendental infinite Bliss.[33]

Kamayani: History, Allegory, and Myth

Prasad insisted on the historicity of *Kamayani* and went to some length to establish it on the basis of ancient scriptures and *Puranas*. He regarded these books as historical documents because history to him was not a mere statement of political events but the biography of a society. To those who regard history as a collection of bare facts, he had this to say:

Today we look upon truth as being facts. Yet we are not satisfied with mere chronology of dates and events but are keen on discerning the psychological import of events through an extensive research of history. What after all is their basic significance? Profound experiences of the soul! Yes. It is this approach alone which gives us insight into the truth of events. Mere events become gross and momentary and fade away into oblivion but the subtler experience or import becomes the abiding truth for ages to follow.[34]

Although Prasad insisted on the historicity of *Kamayani*, he was willing to regard it as an allegorical commentary on human civilization. The episodes presented in *Kamayani*, he says in his preface, are so old that allegory has inevitably crept in. "Therefore," he continues, "I have no objection to Manu, Shradha, and Ida functioning symbolically also."[35]

Prasad's understatement has not gone unnoticed as *Kamayani* has, in fact, generally been interpreted as an allegory about the rise and growth of human civilization. "*Kamayani*," according to

Lodha, "presents a psychological interpretation of human history—not racial, not material, but the basic conflict of man—his littleness and limitedness, follies and faults of his life and the continuous struggle he is involved in. The base of *Kamayani* is historical, sociological, anthropological and above all psychological in its structure."[36]

The symbolism is quite clear. The main events of the epic at the symbolic level, according to Shukla, are defeat of selfish ego, first union of man and woman, the development of civilization through the love of man and woman, the unbridled possessiveness of man giving rise to physical conflict, excessive reliance on reason, the defeat of pure reason, and the victory of *Samrasa* ["Harmony"].[37]

Manu, symbolic of the human psyche, is divided between love and forgiveness, represented by Kamayani, and pure reason, symbolized by Ida. He sets out to start a civilization and what happens to him is the story of human civilization. He starts with the help of faith, love, and cooperation, but is soon dazzled and taken in by the blinding superficial efficiency of reason to such an extent that he finds it impossible to return to love and faith and forgiveness, his initial capital. The interest gets so high that the principal is lost in the shuffle. *Kamayani* is an allegorical search for the balanced mode of existence and Manu merely takes the archetypal steps. The paradise is lost not because the fruit is forbidden but because it is neglected. It is regained toward the end because the victim, Kamayani, rises above herself and forgives him who knows not. There is no external Christ in the book: the Eve of *Kamayani* plays that role. There is no God in this *Paradise Lost,* but only the divine Kamayani, who pursues the very human Manu, for it is he who must walk the tightrope of trial and error and help her create Manav, her son.[38]

The rather obvious symbolic connections of *Kamayani* could easily reduce it to a heavy-handed allegory; but, fortunately, the drama is played out and, for the most part, not directly narrated or commented upon. The symbols have full human personalities, and the language of *Kamayani* skillfully combines the human

The Epic Voice: Kamayani

and the sensuous with the metaphorical and allegorical. Here, for example, is Ida:

> Tresses like tangled logic twined
> Her forehead was clear like the silvery moon
> Akin to the dazzling crown of the world
> Her lotus-like eyes like cups of wine.[39]

The dazzling clarity, the seductive temptation, and the fatal logicality of Reason all become part of the metaphorical description of Ida.

Kamayani's first appearance on the scene, on the other hand, is described in an entirely different way:

> Her innermost charm was joyously expressed,
> In her carefree, graceful figure;
> Like a sapling, playing with the breeze,
> So very lovely and full of fragrance.[40]

Or, to take a far more comparable verse:

> Curly locks supported on shoulders,
> Had densely clustered around her face,
> Like those sprightly babes of clouds,
> Rushing to the moon for collecting nectar.[41]

"Curly," yes; "tangled," no. The contrast between Reason and Faith is quite naturally incorporated within the very appearances of Ida and Kamayani.

Manu, however, is introduced to us as caught in a complex conflict:

> Although beaming with perfect manhood,
> His body alas! was anxiety-smitten,
> While deep within his neglected youth,
> Flowed the lucid stream, so sweet.[42]

and left to ask himself: "How long should I be brooding on/The ruined race of reckless gods?/Will the immortal also die?"[43] The end of his brooding in the first canto is only a prologue to a long and tragic journey undertaken to answer the question: "Will the mortal rise?"

The main concern of *Kamayani* is the creation of a perfect universe. The stage on which this drama is enacted is truly cosmic. Manu sets out on his task against the backdrop of elemental forces of nature, present in their naked glory and overwhelming largeness:

> Earth, like a gasping tortoise, was swaying
> Helter-skelter in helpless plight.
>
> The dreadful lashing of wailing waters
> Was fast advancing like unbridled passions;
> The cyclonic storms of disastrous doom
> Were ardently caressing intense darkness.[44]

Even the traces of old units of measurement cannot be found and Manu has to confront an entirely different scale:

> Stars and planets in the great commotion
> Appeared like paltry, minute bubbles;
> In tumultuous showers of deadly doom,
> They were twinkling like specky glow-worms.[45]

The enormous task Manu faces is nothing less than defeating the dark forces both within and without. The very first indication of hope is presented through the metaphor of a battle:

> Usha[46] dawned like the Victorious Lakshmi[47]
> Throwing golden arrows all around
> The defeated night of doom retreated
> And sank in the recesses of the deep.[48]

The forces of nature participate fully in the drama in which Manu is both an actor and director, or, to put it another way, Manu

The Epic Voice: Kamayani

and his fellow actors frequently seem to be only duplicating the drama nature is playing on its own. Manu and Kamayani, for example, merely reenact the drama of courtship nature has already played:

> On the ocean-bed now sat the Earth,
> Like a shy and bashful bride;
> Deeply wounded in her mind,
> By insolent memories of the doomsday night.[49]

The close connection between the drama of emotions directed by Manu and the drama directed by Nature is not simply a case of extended pathetic fallacy but a clear indication of the far-reaching, cosmic consequences of Man's first attempts to carve out a culture for himself. The injured pride of the bride described above is not a reflection of human emotion but a warning regarding what Manu will end up doing to Kamayani much later in the book. Nature in *Kamayani* does not imitate Man, but helps reinforce the grave implications of what he does.

Kamayani abounds in exquisitely appropriate descriptions of Nature. Here, for example, is Prasad's description of a calm sky:

> The sky was like a bowl of Sapphire,
> Obversely hanging devoid of *Soma*;[50]
> Today the wind was softly breathing,
> As though the perils had fully ceased.[51]

Nature in *Kamayani* is, however, not always quiet and beautiful. Her destructive power is also captured with equal force:

> There did thunder the ocean-waves,
> Like fatal snares of cruel time;
> Emitting deadly foams of poison
> Like serpents spreading dreadful hoods.[52]

The key element in these descriptions is their appropriateness.

They form parts of a tightly structured interplay between the human and the superhuman forces in *Kamayani*.

Prasad's uncanny ability to capture and describe subtle human emotions and passions, an essentially lyrical quality, gives *Kamayani* its memorable verses in which Prasad has described some of the most fundamental human sentiments. Here is Kamayani's slightly reluctant admission of having enjoyed her submission to Manu:

> Eyelids were gently drooping, while the
> Tip of the nose stooped down;
> Her creeper like eye-brows were climbing
> Right up to the ears.
> Her shyness had started touching,
> Her lovely cheeks and ears,
> It blossomed like the *Kadamba*[53] flowers
> Her voice was choked with emotion.[54]

The gamut of emotions described in *Kamayani* ranges from bashfulness, "that comely expression which rightly adorns the rosy ears,"[55] to utter despondency, which forces Manu to invite self-oblivion to come and "Surround me with sorrow."[56]

The most philosophical of his works, *Kamayani* is Prasad's most serious effort to deal with some of the most fundamental questions of life. It examines the place of Faith and Reason in life, and presents a critique of Man's lopsided efforts to come up with the final solution.

Kamayani is quite clearly a critique of pure reason and the mechanized, industrial society it can give rise to. The failure of the rationalistic, industrial civilization managed by Ida and Manu is an expression of that disapproval. Manu is unable to hold his own because Reason alone is not enough. It is, however, equally against self-centered emotionalism as exemplified by Manu. It represents Prasad's search for a genuine compromise between the loving faith of Kamayani and the dazzling rationalism of Ida.

The Language of *Kamayani*

Prasad's distinctive language finds a natural home in the serious epic concerns of *Kamayani*. He has sometimes been criticized for using a uniformly Sanskritized language that creates some unnaturalness in his stories, plays, and novels, where all his characters seem to speak alike. The deliberately archaic and heavily Sanskritized language, however, seems to be just the right medium for *Kamayani*, an epic that reaches far back into prehistory. The attention devoted to the language of *Kamayani* by Prasad is responsible for the numerous corrections in the manuscript.

It is difficult to capture the flavor of the language of *Kamayani* in translation since English translations invariably come out lacking the smooth flow of the verses of *Kamayani* that seem to glide into each other.[57] "The chief characteristic of the language of *Kamayani*," says Singh, "is its systematic avoidance of harsh sounds."[58]

Native Hindi analysts of *Kamayani*'s language, in their enthusiasm for taxonomizing uses of language according to tradition, have classified the linguistic devices employed by Prasad, entirely missing the point. Instead of studying the relationship of these linguistic devices with the meanings expressed by them, they provide classifications that seem pointless. Gupta, for example, devotes an entire book to the language of *Kamayani*, but all that he does is to provide examples of grammatical violations recognized by Indian theorists of poetic language.[59] He cites, for example, many violations of grammatical gender in *Kamayani*, and although he realizes that Prasad may have used some grammatically feminine words in the masculine to emphasize the point of view adopted by him, he does not exploit the suggestion but merely concludes: "It is, therefore, clear that the use of gender is a matter of personal choice."[60] Admittedly, it is; but a personal choice entails certain stylistic implications.

Singh is also insensitive to the implications of various deletions he so painstakingly catalogues as instances of ungrammaticality.[61] Although Gupta and Singh are willing to permit some of them for reasons of rhyme and meter, their guiding principle is still the one laid down by Dwivedi, the neoclassicist Prasad reacted against: "Rules of grammar should not be ignored in poetry. Grammatically correct language commands more respect than grammatically incorrect language."[62]

That a new sensibility can be expressed with a language that conforms completely to older canons of diction and syntax is, to say the least, an unsafe critical assumption. The language of *Kamayani* is a direct refutation of such an assumption. What is more important, however, is that its stylistic innovations are organically related to its thematic and philosophical concerns.

The language of the canto entitled "Lust" ["Vasana"], for example, pays little attention to gender agreement: a fairly straightforward iconic reflection of the obliteration of gender distinction when both parties become one.[63]

That ungrammaticality is not used as a tour de force should be obvious from the remarkable restraint Prasad shows thoroughout *Kamayani*. To heighten sensibilities with suggestive language and not to shock them with deliberately unconventional diction and imagery is, in fact, the guiding principle of *Kamayani*. Here is Prasad's description of sexual union between Manu and Shradha:

> And again the impatient passionate kiss,
> Which sets impetuous blood to flame,
> Cool and patient breaths were quickened
> For quenching thirst of erotic desires.
>
> In between those wooden sticks,
> In that solitary cozy cave,
> Fiery flame quietly quelled down
> Like happy dreams on waking.[64]

The development of Prasad from his first major work, *Tears*, to *Dhruvaswamini* is clearly duplicated in the growth-pattern of *Kamayani*. The manuscript of *Kamayani* contains numerous corrections and modifications, some dated. Most of the dated corrections

The Epic Voice: Kamayani

are, however, from before the publication of *Skandgupta* and *One Sip*. The first three cantos of the epic contain far more corrections than the last few. As Prasad matures from the sentimental author of the first edition of *Tears* to the confident creator and subtle craftsman of its revised version, *Kamayani* flows more smoothly and surely. An examination of these corrections and modifications is very revealing, and leads to the same conclusions that a comparative study of *Ajatshatru* and *Skandgupta* or of the two editions of *Tears* might.

The manuscript changes fall chiefly into the following categories: (1) deletions, (2) changes in word order, (3) changes in diction, and (4) rearrangement of lines. Deletions are extremely revealing. They show Prasad's concern for the rather thin line between sensuousness and sensuality. They clearly indicate that although he is a sensuous poet, he prefers to operate under certain constraints, and that he is not interested in shock techniques but in restoring genuinely poetic expression of deeply felt emotions. If the linguistic choices appear a bit compromising at times, it is because a compromise between the individual and the tradition is in fact the major accomplishment of Prasad: he wants to express individual sensibility without depriving the individual of the richness of the tradition. The changes in word order exhibit a remarkable concern, present also in the revision of *Tears*, for rhythm, emphasis, and the internal phonological structure of the line. The changes in diction also contribute to a greater uniformity of the lexicon.

Another important fact to note is that although there are some manuscript changes in the last four cantos, none of them involves deletions of whole lines or rearrangements of blocks of lines, a clear indication of a surer control both of the narrative and the language employed.

Kamayani: A Summing Up

An overall evaluation of a work such as *Kamayani* is not an easy matter. Since it touches on so many things, it has been the subject of quite a few literary controversies. "There is," says Lal, "nothing quite like *Kamayani* in the whole range of Hindi literature."[65] Although most Hindi critics acknowledge it to be the greatest work of Modern Hindi, some have taken issue with its allegedly escapist philosophical orientation. The criticism, made most tellingly by Muktibodh, is that Prasad is really not able to resolve the conflicts raised in the book, and that Manu's retreat is, in fact, an admission of defeat. "Manu," he says, "is a child of defeat, who tries to hide his failure by escaping."[66]

Kamayani must not, however, be analyzed as a play or a novel. Muktibodh makes the mistake of looking at it as an anthology of character sketches. He does not like Manu's pleasure-seeking capitalism, Shradha's excessive individualism, and Ida's nationalism. But *Kamayani* is a poem and not a gallery of linguistically painted portraits.

It is interesting to note that Muktibodh's criticism is directed almost exclusively against *Kamayani*. He has high praise for other works of Prasad: "Guided by a strong individualistic sensibility, Prasad has created dignified and likeable characters in his plays and short-stories. The idealism of these characters is based on the strength of human relationships. Prasad's strong side finds its expression in his plays and short-stories and not in *Kamayani*."[67]

Muktibodh's positive evaluation of works other than *Kamayani* raises the distinct possibility that he has perhaps misinterpreted the very nature of *Kamayani*. He interprets it sometimes as a novel and sometimes as a play and finds it lacking in what he finds in abundance in Prasad's fictional and dramatic works.

Having dealt with human existence in the historical perspective as in his short stories and plays and in the contemporary socio-political perspective as in his short stories and novels, Prasad turns to the creation of a utopia in *Kamayani* and it must not be judged in terms irrelevant for the evaluation of a utopia. As a matter of fact, *Kamayani* itself criticizes the human tendencies Muktibodh finds so offensive. His criticism of Manu appears pale and meaningless when we consider the fact that the main point of *Kamayani* is to depict the defeat of Manu's selfish individualism, and the criticism he makes of Ida can hardly match her self-evaluation:

The Epic Voice: Kamayani

> Today I find I am so very poor,
> I do not even like myself at all;
> Whatever songs I happen to sing,
> I am not able to hear them at all.[68]

Muktibodh also objects, and here he is not alone, to the last canto of the book on the ground that it does not seem to be an integral part of it, but merely tagged on as a philosophical, and not dramatic, imperative. The book ends on a compromise, and compromises never quite feel comfortable, structurally or otherwise.

Prasad does, however, try to provide some structural unity. It is significant to note that Manu ends up where he began: in a remote corner of the Himalayas. The concluding lines of the poem seem almost a repetition of the opening lines. *Kamayani* opens with a description of "one primal energy, matter or life, whatever the name,"[69] and concludes: "Matter and life were harmonious/Exquisite was the form of beauty."[70]

The circle has been completed. Manu's task was not to sustain himself in the world he helped created but to withdraw from it after creating it. Manu, Kamayani, and Ida are all rather like actors that must retreat when the curtain falls. They let us see the pitfalls they went through and the false steps they took.

The last canto is the final statement of the utopia:

> Man is the witness of consciousness,
> He smiles without any blemish,
> In sweet communion with his heart
> He appears to dive still deeper.
>
> Forget all dividing barriers,
> Be serene in joys and sorrows,
> Oh! Man, proclaim "I am this,"
> This world becomes one family.[71]

Defending *Kamayani* against the charge that it tends to appeal to "a salon kind of escapist spiritual interest," Lal correctly observes that the objection is "irrelevant" because it is admittedly "a sophisticated poem," meant for "the sophisticated and the leisured."[72]

"*Kamayani*," says Sahney, "is an epic, but it is unique in many respects and stands apart in its own pre-eminence from all other specimens of the kind. It is not a narrative poem like other epics, though it has a very interesting story to tell. It is perhaps the most lyrical epic in style as well as in substance, in style because it is written in rhyme and stanzaic schemes, in substance because it is distinguished throughout by an unprecedented intensity of emotion and imagination. It is perhaps the most musical, the most passionate, and the most imaginative of the world's epics."[73] He goes on to compare it with epics like the *Faerie Queene* and the *Divine Comedy* and concludes that *Kamayani* is "the most metaphysical and mystical long poem in the world's literature."[74]

In spite of the fact that *Kamayani* can be compared with almost any major epic, its nature and structure suggest that it is, as argued by Gautam, more like Plato's *Republic* and More's *Utopia* than the epics it compares favorably with.[75]

Chapter Eight
Postscript

Fiction

Kamayani, Prasad's masterpiece, was followed by the publication of *The Web* [*Indrajal*], a collection of fourteen short stories, first published in 1936; *Iravati*, a novel; and *Poetry and Art and Other Essays* [*Kavya aur Kala tatha Anya Nibandh*], a collection of critical essays. The last two were published posthumously.

Written during the composition period of *Kamayani*, the short stories of *The Web* show remarkable restraint and control. "Gangster" ["Gunda"] is perhaps the best-known story from this collection.

It is the story of Nanku Singh, a gang leader devoted to protecting the poor and the weak. He takes it upon himself to punish Kubra, the Muslim agent of the white regiment in Banaras, when he tries to take advantage of Dulari. The information reaches Panna Devi, who had once loved Nanku but was forced to marry Prince Balwant Singh. Nanku finds out that the British are planning to move Panna Devi to Calcutta and takes it upon himself to help the queen and her family escape. In the process, however, he is attacked and killed.

The forthright simplicity of its style is truly compelling. Made up almost entirely of simple sentences, it virtually attacks the reader. Here is the opening paragraph:

He was more than fifty. Even then he was more powerful and determined than young men. There were no wrinkles in his skin. In pouring rain, in the cold nights of December, and in the hot days of June, he enjoyed moving about without many clothes on. His waxed moustaches like the stings of a scorpion challenged everyone. His black skin was bright and slithery like that of a snake. The red border of his long skirt drew attention even from a distance.[1]

"The Chariot of the Gods" ["Deva-ratha"] and "Doubt" ["Sandeh"] are also, like "The Gangster," penetrating character studies of their central figures. They show a very mature Prasad dealing effectively and dramatically with complex human predicaments.

"The Chariot of the Gods" is the story of Sujata, a Buddhist *deva-dasi* ("temple girl"), who refuses to believe that life is not real. She is, however, not alone. Her lover, Aryamitra, tells her that he has told the rector of the monastery that he had become a monk only to pursue her and would like to marry her if she is willing to opt out of Buddhism. She cannot, she says, though she does love him. Aryamitra does not quite understand her logic, until he is told that she does not want to become his wife because her body has been committed to the Lord. Though Aryamitra is willing to ignore this datum, she is not. The conversation is overheard by the rector, who interprets her admission of love for Aryamitra as heresy and sentences her to death. Sujatra's response has to be one of the most brutal attacks on Buddhism of her day: "Even the cruelest of deaths would be a pleasure. There is nothing left for me on this affectionate planet, rector. Your religious rule destroys homes in order to create sanctuaries—imprisons life in illusion. You destroy holy family relationships in order to create the home of your desires. The only difference is you give it another name. Your lust is actually not even as noble as that of an ordinary man."[2]

"Doubt" is a character study of a slightly different kind. It is the story of Shyama, a strong-minded religious widow, and a rather clever man who secretly loves her for her puritanism. He thinks he is loved by a married woman, but he is not attracted by her as

Postscript

she violates his sense of morality. Unfortunately, he cannot see the paradox he has created for himself. One day, he threatens to leave and Shyama discovers he has a picture of her with him. The widow realizes that what he really needs is a mother: "Loving is not easy. You don't understand this game. So, don't waste your time. Yes, a woman in trouble is calling you and you should go and help her. Help her and come back. All your stuff will be here when you come back. You have to stay here. Do you understand? You need my guardianship. Come on, get up!"[3] The strength and self-confidence of Shyama remind one of the princess in *Rajyashri*. She is a rational and mature human being, qualities generally not attributed to women in Modern Hindi literature (not to say anything about how they are treated in Medieval Hindi literature).

Whereas "The Gangster," "The Chariot of the Gods," and "Doubt" are character studies, "Nuri," "Salvati," and "Painted Rocks" ["Chitravale Patthar"] are evocative stories dedicated to creating a mood and an atmosphere. They abound in evocative descriptions like the following from "Nuri": "This wonderful creation of the Mughal Empire! The golden dream of Akbar's Youth, the fort of Fatehpur Sikri, lay scattered on the rocks. Such a sudden rise and such a sudden decline! Right where the birth of a new religion was announced the strengths and the shortcomings of Christianity, Zoroastrianism, Jainism, Islam, and Hinduism were discussed, right where the holy shrine of Salim was, and right where Prince Salim was born, lay the scattered fort of Sikri, widowed even during Akbar's own life-time."[4]

The impact of the intellectual and philosophical preoccupations of *Kamayani* is clearly visible in the short stories of *The Web*. The language is more refined and intellectualized. In "Comma" ["Viram Chinha"], for example, the end of the old woman who insists on carrying the dead body of her son into the temple that had been blocked off for him and his associates is described in the concluding lines of the story in a style that is clearly a mark of later years: "Radhe's dead body was rested just near the entrance.

The old woman bowed her head, but could not lift it. For the untouchables trying to enter the temple, she stayed there as a comma."[5]

But the past was what he felt most comfortable with and his last attempt at the novel, *Iravati*, took him back to the period of Indian history he knew best. *Iravati*, an incomplete historical romance, was published posthumously in 1936.

Its central figure is Iravati, a religious dancer, who is ordered to spend her life in a Buddhist monastery by a king. She finds life in the monastery stifling and escapes. Her love of life and beauty are counterpointed against their negation as institutionalized by a declining Buddhism. The main characters and events are drawn from history, and the reconstruction of contemporary life is authentic.

Iravati is a dancer and she must dance to celebrate the beauty of life and nature. She takes the Buddhist obsession with sin to task when a colleague tells her that she cannot praise the beauty of the night. When a monk says: "As the beauty of the night can excite one sexually, my friend, its description is prohibited," she retorts: "What? This festival of the moon, and you can't even praise it. Tonight is a night to dance. You are simply enumerating your weaknesses. No. I am innocent. I only worship my life, which is as clean as the moonlight. I shall dance to celebrate."[6]

Iravati seeks to present the conflict between the purity and vitality of the innocent Iravati and the ritual-ridden Brahmanism on the one hand and the life-denying negativism of Buddhism on the other. The king accuses her of being a prostitute, but it is he who is trying to secure her for his harem. The facade of moral integrity is obvious enough, but the king, in a moment of weakness, even says so: "Iravati, I couldn't understand myself. Your dance swept me off my feet. I thought that was not art but poison, that could kill hundreds. But that was my excuse."[7] The chief of the monastery, who imposes disciplinary rules, is not unaware of the fact that Iravati is there because the ruler wants her for himself eventually. Iravati is, however, an artist, committed to life and beauty and not easily intimidated. When she is taken prisoner, she tells the friend who offers to help: "I have danced before gods. Now I want to see what the ungodly can make me do."[8]

Convinced of her innocence, Iravati takes up one challenge after another and exposes the corrupt motives of the self-styled guardians of peace and religion. She becomes a symbol of life in a society that seems to be courting death. The total denial of man's creative energy represented by people around her can only spell the hypocrisy of self-annihilation. As Prasad himself observes in the preface: "Man has destroyed civilizations and reconstructed them. A picture almost complete can be ruined. Artificiality can create incompatibility even among perfectly measured strokes. Then the artist has to begin all over again, and then he comes up with something beautiful. Trying to make something too perfect can sometimes lead to ugliness, and then he comes up with something beautiful. Trying to make something too perfect can also lead to ugliness, and then we must break away from it. Our non-violence has become our destroyer; our love now hates us; and our religion has become sin."[9]

Iravati demonstrates how. Her commitment to her art is not tolerated by a religion that teaches tolerance; her loyalty and devotion to herself are construed as corruption by a religion that emphasizes perfection; her love of life is interpreted as destruction by those who think they are engaged in the business of maintaining a great civilization. The ironies are manifold and the novel exploits them to their full extent.

It becomes a reexamination of values and tenets that find expression in Prasad's earlier works. The priest of the temple where Iravati used to dance says: "Our truth has become weak. We will have to renew it. We will have to revive the vital forces of our culture. Our cowardice allows us to rationalize too much. Our culture, pretending not to hurt anyone, is destroying life itself. I am confident we will have to restore values we, in our rationalism, abandoned as harmful."[10]

Human energy must be allowed to create; to deny its basic right is to kill it. The point is repeatedly emphasized in *Iravati*. The willingness to put up with almost anything is tantamount to accepting a dangerously destructive definition of Man. The priest asks: "Is Magadha the only such unfortunate country with so many poor philosophers? One who doesn't have clothes is only too willing to think that man is born without them. That becomes a principle, and people walk around naked. If you swallow an insect accidentally, you blame yourself for its demise and tape your mouth!"[11]

Iravati is in many ways an attempt to answer the problem raised by *Kamayani*. Kamayani gives too much and allows her traditional role to be exploited. Iravati not only defines her own role but also defends it with vitality against the forces of death and decay around her. Innocent and kind as Kamayani, Iravati is not willing to let the spark of life be extinguished by ritualistic ashes that hide a multitude of sins. Assertive and confident of her innocence, it is impossible for her to succumb. She must survive so that the human spirit can survive.

The destruction of morality's hollow empire run by the king who has Iravati imprisoned is brought about, ironically but justifiably enough, by Kalindi, the beautiful young woman his father wanted to seduce. The old king's death puts her in isolation, and she seeks out her revenge. The real decadence is not in Iravati but in those who cannot rise above their own obsession with sin. They are obsessed with sin because they are inherently capable of far more sin than an artist merely devoted to perfecting her art.

The novel, clearly Prasad's best, is, unfortunately, incomplete. But even as an incomplete piece, it gives what *The Skeleton* and *Titali* lack. The background of ancient history provides Prasad the confidence he lacks in the contemporary pieces. His decision to abandon contemporary themes, dealt with far more effectively by Prem Chand, allowed him to not only create what is undoubtedly a first-rate novel but also to fill a gap in Hindi literature: *Iravati* is the first historical novel in Hindi.

Literary Criticism

During the last few years of his life, Prasad also wrote some serious literary criticism. The eight articles written during this period were collected and published posthumously in 1937 under the title *Poetry and Art and Other Essays* [*Kavya aur Kala tatha anya Nibandh*]. Indicative of his profound scholarship and his familiarity with the almost entire range of Sanskrit literature, these essays reveal a sensitive and critical mind.

"Poetry and Art" ["Kavya aur Kala"] is concerned with the definition and classification of poetry and with finding Indian antecedents of the proposed definition. Prasad is chiefly concerned with finding traditional sanctions for what he has to propose: "Even the learned critics are bent upon arguing that Chhayavad (Romanticism) and Rahasyavad (Mysticism) are alien and that the modern Hindi tendency to create inanimate objects as if they were conscious being comes from English. This is so because most critics have harped on the tune that whatever is new in Hindi is necessarily a foreign element."[12]

He goes on to show that quite a bit of what is considered to be alien or foreign is in fact deeply rooted in the tradition that Hindi literature is so unmistakably a part of.

He defines poetry as an expression of the ultimate synthesis and regards it as the highest form of spiritualism. Since God in the Indian tradition is both abstract and concrete, poetry, he argues, cannot be considered different from other more abstract forms of spiritualism.

The essay is an explicit plea for the construction of an Indian aesthetics. An aesthetics based on traditional concepts does not, he points out, artificially establish local values over those that may be considered universal. It merely makes the interpretation of what is necessarily an exploitation of local circumstances that much more meaningful. The search for such an aesthetics is not only relevant but also necessary. He cites an anecdote according to which Shahjahan misinterprets the poetic conventions employed by a poet and has to be corrected by a courtier and observes: "If we do not keep the Indian context in mind when evaluating our literature, we are likely to be guilty of the same thing as Shahjahan."[13]

He returns to the theme of finding traditional Indian antecedents of mysticism and romanticism in "Mysticism" ["Rahasyavad"] and "Realism and Romanticism" ["Yatarthavad and Chhayavad"]. In the former, he argues that mysticism is not only native but also the central component of the great Indian poetic tradition: "The non-dualistic mysticism of modern Hindi literature is an integral and entirely natural development of mysticism in Indian literature. It is an effort to harmonize the individual with the universe he is a part of with the help of subtle imagery and description of the beauty of nature. Of course, separation, as a counterpoint of union, joins in, as is entirely appropriate given the contemporary context. That modern mysticism is India's own heritage cannot be doubted."[14]

"Realism and Romanticism" is devoted to a definition of *chayavad*, the school of poetry inaugurated by Prasad, and to realism and its place in the Indian tradition. Aware of the allegations that Chhayavad was an un-Indian return to nature and a deliberate seeking out of ambiguities, Prasad sets the record straight by pointing out that romanticism has perfectly respectable antecedents in traditional Indian literature and that it is neither a search for ambiguities nor a return to nature. He argues: "Some consider a deliberate search for ambiguities essential to Chhayavad. It is possible that such results obtain only when the poet fails to understand what he is talking about, to express himself in a systematic fashion, to choose the right diction, or to internalize his intellectual perceptions. But from this it cannot be argued that vagueness, abstractness, and ambiguity characterize Chhayavad."[15]

Neither can Chhayavad be identified with a return to nature. Although nature has become more than an accidental ingredient of modern Hindi poetry, he argues, it cannot be maintained that poetry dealing with nature is necessarily Chhayavad poetry. It is surely possible to find nature poetry that is not modern in the intended sense.

After extensively documenting the existence of what he calls Chhayavad in ancient Indian literature, he returns to the allegation that it is un-Indian and concludes: "Chhayavad had established itself in ancient Indian literature. When similar experiments began in Hindi, some people were surprised. But they were, in spite of their opposition, forced to accept this form of expression. Needless to say such deeply felt personalized expressions were necessary. They were not merely rhetorical games, like those of Kaku and Shlesh. Poetry has withdrawn to the inner universe."[16]

As far as the opposition between Chhayavad and realism is concerned, Prasad believes that a poet is neither a historian nor a priest, but someone who fills the gap between religion and history. Although he offers a seasoned defense of realism by observing that it is un-Indian and concludes: "Chhayavad has established pain and sorrow around him, his sympathy clearly lies with romanticism. Realism, he observes, has found the medium of prose, presumably implying that it may not be the right content for verse. He is very eloquent about the motivations that underlie realistic literature. But his praise for such literature itself is rather limited.

The essay entitled "Rasa" deals with general aesthetic questions, particularly the place of the doctrine of *rasa* in the history of Indian literature. It is a learned account of the theory of *rasa* and shows Prasad's mastery not only of the creative literature of ancient India but also the critical literature devoted to the doctrine of *rasa*.

Three of the essays in the collection are devoted to the theory, history, and practice of drama. In "The Use of Rasa in Drama" ["Natakon me Rasa Ka Prayog"], Prasad argues that traditional Indian aesthetics regards literature as truth and not as imitation of nature. The doctrine of *rasa* is responsible for the emphasis on union and happiness in Indian drama.

In "The Beginnings of Drama" ["Natakon ka Arambh"], Prasad traces the beginnings of Indian drama to Vedic dialogues.

Prasad contends that Vedic dialogues of the following sort must have given rise to drama:

> You, soma-merchant! Want to sell your soma?
> It's for sale.
> Then it will be bought.
> Go ahead.[17]

"Stage" ["Rangamanch"] is another scholarly essay on the place of the stage in classical Indian dramatics. The subject is, according to Prasad, extensively discussed in traditional dramatics. He attempts to reconstruct the stage as described in traditional sources and argues that there are no grounds for believing, as some apparently do, that Indian theater borrowed the device of the curtain from the Greeks.

In "Stage," he also examines the belief that characters in a play should speak a language natural to them. Since the charge that all his characters speak a uniformly High Hindi has been leveled against him, it is interesting to quote his response in full: "I would say that language should reflect the feelings and emotions of the characters in the play. But this should not allow us to break the linguistic unity of the medium employed and employ a cocktail of languages."[18]

Although Prasad's critical writings do not constitute a novel and profound literary theory, his insistence on a reexamination of the past to seek out new justifications for apparently modern and contemporary theories firmly establishes him as a traditionalist of the most romantic sort. His literature is an expression par excellence of the new sensibility, but he takes pains to show that the new sensibility is in fact an integral part of the tradition, if tradition is reconstructed in an undistorted fashion. Real romanticism lies not in merely throwing away the tradition, but in reconstructing it. Prasad's literary criticism is a systematic effort to reconstruct an undistorted picture of the great Indian tradition he so clearly felt a part of. He is anxious to show that his own "innovations"

The Music of Prasad

Iravati was followed by *The Music of Prasad* [*Prasad Sangit*], posthumously published in 1956 with an introduction by Prasad's son, Ratna Shankar Prasad. It contains his sonnets, most of them published in *Indu* during 1912–1916, the songs from his plays, lyrics from *The Waterfall*, one patriotic lyric from *Flowers of the Garden*, a lyric each from *The Wave* and *The House of Pity*, and three new pieces. "In this volume," according to the editor, "father's sonnets and all the songs from his plays have been collected."[19] The miscellaneous pieces included all seem to be prayers meant to be sung.

Though not much is new in *The Music of Prasad*, it underlines the musical quality of his work and provides us with an opportunity to examine his dramatic songs as independent lyrics. Within the plays, they have to be evaluated in terms of their functional integration, and it does not take much away from Prasad to say that they don't all achieve the same degree of functional integration. *The Music of Prasad*, however, allows us to look at them anew as eminently singable lyrical gems.

These songs, as is to be expected, cover a very wide gamut of feelings and emotions, ranging from the fake anger of Kamana— "Go, friend, don't bother me"[20]—to the profound anguish of Skandgupta, who is forced to mock the words of God and challenge Him to live up to His promise:

> When will you unburden us all?
> Didn't you repeatedly say: "I shall reappear in another shape?"[21]
> Limitless pain overwhelms this Earth
> And the Devil licks his bloody tongue.[22]

While some songs in the collection, such as "The Nightingale Sings in the Garden of Youth Today," "How Hard Is the Flame of Youth," and "Oh Youth! Your Unstable Shadow," sing of youth and love in the lighter vein, a majority of them provide memorable words to express the various shades of sorrow. Their haunting melodies capture the sadness of a dissatisfied soul ("My hope is restless today/My thirst has never been quenched"[23]), the desperation of one overwhelmed with sorrow ("Dear friend! What is pleasure?"[24]), the determination of a crushed heart ("Don't you ever cry!"[25]), the questioning of self-reliance ("Have courage enough to row?"[26]), the sense of hopelessness ("Life goes by/Like a game of light and shadow"[27]), and the inability to cope with the burdens of love ("How does one cope with love?"[28]). Music, both of rhythm and diction, is not only the main ingredient of these songs but also the storehouse of their imagery:

> Do not pull the strings of the veena anymore
> Heartless finger! do stop now,
> Be kind for a moment or two,
> This outcry, this stunned strain,
> Will come out senseless.
> Do not tinker with the silent instrument,
> Or disturb the profound silence—
> Lest in the void of the empty air
> The rhythm should scatter meaningless.[29]

Some of the pieces in the collection are what might be called modern *prathanas* ("prayers" or "hymns") and *bhajans* (religious songs chanted in praise of God).[30] They show not only Prasad's religiosity but also his affinity with the saint-poets of the *Bhakti* period. Some of them achieve the same profound simplicity one notices in the religious songs of the *Bhakti* poets:

> Play your flute, Mohan! Please!
> Awaken our dormant lives!
> Say the *mantra* of unstained liberty
> And release us from our bondages![31]

Prasad is, however, not beyond challenging his God. In the following lines from a song from *Kamana*, the singer, like Skandgupta, reminds God to play fair:

> Have fun, playing the game you created!
> But don't isolate yourself as a King and don't be aloof,
> For the world will pay you back, forgetting all kindness.
> Humanity disappears as the creeper of distrust grows
> Sorrow, darkness, and evil, let us eliminate them.[32]

These songs tend to be moralistic and didactic, but as *bhajans* they almost have to be. Their achievement lies in the fact that they are not crushed under the weight of their moralizing but are able to carry it with ease and melody. Essentially devotional in nature they are, in the words of Ramsaran, "confessionals of the soul."[33] The ironic twist seen in the challenges to God quoted above gives them a refreshingly modern touch.

Some of these religious pieces are very short and are rather like *mantras* (chanted in order to assure purity and peace). Pieces like the following are a modern poet's incantations for peace:

> Let Piety rain!
> Drenching this pain-scorched Earth.
> Let Love flow, and forgiveness,
> Eliminating disunity and bringing Peace.[34]

Another group of songs, taken mostly from Prasad's historical plays, is devoted to celebrating India's beauty and its glorious heritage. Since some of these songs have already been discussed in connection with *Skandgupta* and *Chandragupta*, we need not dwell on them here. They underline the thematic concerns of plays like *Chandragupta* and have the fast-moving rhythm that characterizes these plays in general. Perhaps the only point that needs to be made here is that the songs that seem to glorify India do not drown songs such as the following:

> Consider the sad fate of your nation!
> Are you ever going to rescue anyone?
> Always a loser, you don't have much now,
> Are you ever going to go all the way?
> Will you ever do anything, or always
> Just cry and ask for help?[35]

The Music of Prasad provides an appropriate coda for a career that peaked with *Kamayani*, a book that does with language practically all that can be done with it. Musicality is a sine qua non of oral poetry, and Prasad's poetry left the oral tradition it drew upon richer than it found it.

Chapter Nine
Conclusion

The importance of Prasad's contribution to Hindi literature cannot be exaggerated. Literary history, like the history of science, is largely a matter of individual writers rejecting old paradigms and providing new ones.[1] Prasad was one such individual. He freed Hindi poetry from its deadening allegiance to the didactic neoclassicism of his predecessors, and gave it a new language in which to express deeply felt emotions and internalized convictions. By practically demonstrating his dictim that poetry was neither religion nor history but something that filled the gap left by both, he opened the door to modernity and brought Hindi literature more in line with other literatures of the world.

He inaugurated the quest for personality that has characterized some of the best achievements of modern Hindi literature. And he did it not by talking about it or by joining any camp but by showing the possibilities himself. What is really remarkable about his achievement is that he utilized the linguistic, philosophical, and historical resources that were held in high esteem by the theorists and literary artists whom he was reacting against. To provide a new language for "the new sensibility," he went not to the earthy dialect forms or to the alien idiom of English, but to the profoundly respected, classical language of Sanskrit. The lexicon of his literature is made up almost entirely of words of Sanskrit origin. The density of Sanskrit words seen in Prasad could have a disastrous effect on a lesser author. Hindi literature abounds with examples of writers who, when they went to Sanskrit, produced punditry instead of poetry. Prasad did not go to Sanskrit in order to appear scholarly but to find raw materials for constructing a language suitable for his needs. The choice of Sanskrit as his main linguistic reservoir underlines his desire to forge a revolution from within the hidden recesses of tradition.

Philosophically, he did not espouse the current and not so current slogans, but chose to reexamine the classics of Indian thought in order to find things that should have been picked up but were, unfortunately, not. In the preface to *Dhruvaswamini*, he argues: "The practical implications of our religion and ethics have not always been consistently interpreted. We are only too inclined to label new reforms and sociological experiments 'un-Indian'. I am, however, convinced that practically all experiments were tried in our long tradition."[2]

He chose to show that what appeared to be new was in fact deeply rooted in tradition and that, therefore, there were really no grounds for rejecting some of the "new" sociological experiments that had to be undertaken to save the society from utter decadence. He was thus a revolutionary in the deepest sense of the word. Search for illumination of the present in terms of the past is what characterizes his dramatic output. The internal segmentation of Indian society and its tragic consequences are effectively captured in plays like *Skandgupta* and *Chandragupta*. These mirrors of history provide a transparent warning to those who would prefer to operate otherwise. These plays, according to Bhatnagar, "revolutionized our historical drama with their dynamic outlook" and are still unsurpassed in "their romantic imagination, poetic exuberance, and cultural themation."[3]

Although the lack of a really alive literary theater prevented successful staging of his plays and although they are generally read rather than performed, they are perfectly stageworthy. The fact that they have never been very popular as stagepieces is a comment on the sad state of theater in India. Prasad himself observed:

My plays should not be compared with the commercial productions of Tulsidatta Shaida and Aga Hashra. I have not written these plays

Conclusion

for theatre companies that collect half-a-dozen actors and a few curtains from anywhere they can get them and move from one place to another to collect nickels and dimes from hawkers, coolies and small shopkeepers. Plays like *Uttar Ramcharita, Shakuntala* and *Mudra Raksas* can never be staged by them nor can they ever inspire the sort of audience these companies seek. Their predominantly poetic style makes some special demands. Polished actors, cultured audiences, and a bit of money, however, can render them very effective.[4]

During Prasad's own career, the dominance of Parasi theatrical companies that, though helpful in reviving theater in India, worked chiefly with plays of little literary value, and the almost total lack of a serious literary stage combined to give his preeminently stageable plays the reputation of being closet dramas. They are not. Although he was, like Shaw, able to create his own audience, he, unlike Shaw, was not enough of a public-relations man to create an adequate literary theater. He can perhaps be faulted for not having promoted the idea of a literary theater. But the fact that he created such dramatic masterpieces as *Dhruwaswamini* and *Skandgupta* in the absence of a literary theater only adds to his stature as a playwright.

A deep understanding of tradition rather than a shallow rejection of it is what distinguishes Prasad from the majority of modern Hindi writers who have more often than not sought out not only their models but also their philosophical commitments in entirely alien sources. His literary output is, in a way, an act of reinterpretation. The desire to reinterpret the entire tradition takes him back to not only ancient history but to the mythic depth of prehistory. This confrontation with the beginning of things, in *Kamayani*, is unique in Hindi, and rare anywhere. He takes up not a legend here and a legend there but the very act of the creation of human civilization as his subject.

He did everything the other major figures of *Chhayavad* did, but went beyond their somewhat localized concerns. He experimented with the formal aspects of poetry and described the personal problems of a romantic sensibility trying to grow up in a ritual-ridden society. Although Nirala ranks higher as an experimenter and Pant higher as the highpriest of nature, none of them has the mythic depth, the philosophical profundity, and the artistic control of Prasad. He, unlike Varma, does not allow poetry to remain at the "I fall upon the thorns of life, I bleed" level, nor does he permit himself metaphysical flashes that do not seem to form part of a consistent philosophical whole. He wrote understandingly, even forcefully, about the poor and the oppressed, but did not accept the hollow claptrap of Marxist poets.

Unlike other major contemporaries, Prasad tried and succeeded in everything. Verma wrote only lyrics and autobiographical essays, Nirala only lyrics and songs, and Pant only lyrics and lyrical narratives. Prasad wrote the lyrics of *The Waterfall* and *The Wave* and the greatest romantic lyric of Hindi, *Tears*. In addition, he gave Hindi the possibility of a truly modern short story, a wealth of dramatic masterpieces, and inaugurated the true historical novel. He has sometimes been compared with another contemporary not associated with Chhayavad, Prem Chand, the author of *The Gift of a Cow* [*Godan*], but Prem Chand's remarkably perceptive realism never left the domain of fiction.

Although formally not as well educated as those he is sometimes compared with, he was clearly the most scholarly of them all. He delved deep into ancient Indian history and mythology, wrote scholarly papers about them, and utilized his findings to anchor the mythic dimensions of *Kamayani*. He is generally compared with nineteenth-century English Romantics, but he is closer to Yeats in that they both attempt to draw on the resources of their respective traditions to construct a new mythology.

Prasad repeatedly broke the barriers generally associated with Romanticism. He wrote, defying Poe's well-known dictum, an exquisitely intense long lyric, *Tears*. He also wrote an epic, a form almost universally construed to be beyond the reach of a Romantic. But what is even more important is that he wrote some of the best drama ever to come out of modern India. The dramatic and the

Conclusion

lyrical do not often go together, but Prasad's literary output is one of those exceptions that is needed to validate the rule.

He not only composed highly successful lyrics and plays but also combined the two supposedly antagonistic modes of aesthetic perception in his work. His better short stories are as dramatic as his epic. The reader is baffled by the objectivity of the plays by the author of *Tears* and the lyrical intensity of the epic by the author of *Skandgupta*.

The hallmark of Prasad's work is synthesis: synthesis of conflicting modes of apprehension, of the clashing demands of the individual and the tradition, and of the opposing claims of history and modernity. He was, to twist Eliot's famous characterization of Arnold a bit, an anticlassical classicist, the best type of romantic.

The growth and development of Prasad are extremely valuable data in any general theory of aesthetic growth. He started out as a lyricist and finished as a novelist. En route, he mastered the dramatic and the epic. His failure as a novelist is instructive, and perhaps has some general implications for our theory. The intensity of the lyricist in him helped him achieve great heights in short fiction. Although it is possible to argue that the novel, which requires nonpoetic, descriptive, sustained narrative, proved to be an alien form for him, the central reason for his failure was perhaps his understandable desire to compete with Prem Chand on the latter's native grounds, the problem-oriented, realistic novel that examines the social structure of contemporary society. The relative success of the unfortunately incomplete *Iravati* suggests very strongly that had he chosen to work on his native grounds, he could have handled the novel with the same success with which he handled the lyric, the drama, and the epic.

Notes and References

Chapter One

1. Khari Boli acquired the status of the chief literary dialect of Hindi during the nineteenth century.
2. Corinne Friend, *Short Stories of Yashpal, Author and Patriot* (Philadelphia: University of Pennsylvania Press, 1969), p. 4. For a good brief survey of Hindi literature, see R. A. Dwivedi, *A Critical Survey of Hindi Literature* (Banaras, 1966).
3. The translation "predominant mood" is just a convenient gloss and does not do full justice to the ancient Indian concept of *rasa*. Sures Chandra Banerji defines it as "an inexplicable inward experience of a connoisseur on witnessing a dramatic performance or reading a poetical composition" (*A Companion to Sanskrit Literature* [Delhi: 1971], p. 452). There is a substantial body of literature devoted to explaining it. For a convenient summary, see K. C. Pandey, *Comparative Aesthetics,* vols. I and II (Varanasi: Chowkhamba, 1959). The traditionally recognized *rasas* are *Shringar* ("erotic"), *Vira* ("heroic"), *Raudra* ("furious"), *Bibhasta* ("disgustful"), *Hasya* ("comic"), *Adbhuta* ("marvelous"), *Karuna* ("pathetic"), and *Bhayankar* ("terrible").
4. Chandra Bardai, *Prithvi Raj Raso,* vi, 39, quoted and translated by John Beames in his *A Comparative Grammar of the Modern Aryan Languages of India,* 2nd Indian reprint (Delhi: Munshiram Manoharlal, 1970), p. 131.
5. Friend, p. 5.
6. Ancient Hindu scriptures.
7. Quoted from Rabindranath Tagore's translation in *One Hundred Poems of Kabir* (London: The India Society, 1915), p. 49. For a more contemporary translation of Kabir's poems, see Robert Bly, *The Kabir Book: Forty Four of the Ecstatic Poems of Kabir* (Boston: Beacon Press, 1977).
8. Friend, p. 5.
9. Quoted from R. T. Gribble's translation in *Mystic Lyrics from*

the Indian Middle Ages (London: Allen and Unwin, 1928), p. 59.

10. Ibid., p. 60. Kabir, it must be emphasized, is not obscure merely for the sake of being obscure. According to John A. Ramsaran, he sees truth "as essentially having a logic contrary to that of ordinary reason" (*English and Hindi Religious Poetry: An Analogical Study* [Leiden, 1973], p. 139).

11. Ibid., p. 39. Most of Tulsidas's religious songs are to be found in *Kavitavali* and *Vinay Patrika*. See F. R. Allchin, tr., *Kavitavali* (London: Allen and Unwin, 1964) and *The Petition to Ram* (London: Allen and Unwin, 1966).

12. Ainslie Embree, *The Hindu Tradition* (New York: Modern Library, 1966), pp. 248–49.

13. Quoted from G. A. Atkins, tr., *The Ramayana of Tulsidas* (Delhi: The Times of India Press, 1954), p. 1143.

14. Ibid., p. 928.

15. Ibid., p. 1318.

16. Ibid., p. 166.

17. Her father's vow was that she should wed the one who could bend Shiva's bow.

18. Atkins, p. 294.

19. Ibid., p. 352.

20. For a detailed discussion of Hindi religious poetry of the *Bhakti* period, see John A. Ramsaran, *English and Hindi Religious Poetry* and Hazari Prasad Dwivedi, *Madhya Kalina Dharm Sadhana* (Allahabad; Sahitya Bhawan, 1962).

21. Friend, p. 6. For a good general introduction to the poetry of this period, see Nagendra, *Riti Kavya Ki Bhumika* (New Delhi: National Publishing House, 1952).

22. Ibid., p. 6.

23. S. H. Vatsyayan, "Hindi Literature," in *Contemporary Indian Literature: A Symposium* (New Delhi, 1959), p. 80.

24. Ronald Stuart McGregor, *Hindi Literature of the Nineteenth and Early Twentieth Centuries* (Wiesbaden, 1974), p. 112.

25. David Rubin, *Selected Poems of Nirala: A Season on the Earth* (New York, 1976), p. 125.

26. Nagendra, *Hindi Sahitya Kosh* (New Delhi: National Publishing House, 1978), p. 325.

27. Vatsyayan, p. 80.

Notes and References

28. Ibid., p. 81.
29. Sushama Pal, *Chhayavad Ki Darshnik Prashthabhumi* (Delhi: National Publishing House, 1971), p. 15. For a particularly well-argued defense of the position that it was Prasad who started it all, see Kishori Lal Gupta, *Prasad ka Vikasatmak Adhyayan* (Allahabad, 1971).
30. Quoted by Gupta, *Prasad,* p. 31.
31. From "The Symphony of Clouds" by Nirala, translated by M. Halpern in Vidya Niwas Misra, ed., *Modern Hindi Poetry: An Anthology* (Bloomington: University of Indiana Press, 1965), p. 58.
32. Jaishankar Prasad, *Ansoo* (Jhansi, 1925), p. 9.
33. Mahadevi Varma, "Preface" to *Rashmi* (Allahabad: Sahitya Bhawan, 1942), p. 7.
34. Mahadevi Varma, *Adhunik Kavi* (Allahabad: Hindi Sahitya Sammelan, 1950), p. 10.
35. Friend, p. 9.
36. For a good general introduction to his work, see Michael Swan, *Munshi Prem Chand of Lamhi Village* (Durham, N.C., 1972).
37. Rubin, p. 126.
38. His Highness the Maharaja of Banaras.
39. B. L. Sahney, tr., "Introduction" to *Kamayani*, by Jaishankar Prasad (New Delhi, 1971), p. 5.
40. *Kavi-Sammelans* are public gatherings in which poets recite their poetry to large audiences, often into the late hours of the morning.
41. Nand Dulare Bajpai, *Jaishankar Prasad,* 2nd ed. (Allahabad, 1966).
42. Sahney, p. 3.
43. Ibid., p. 7.
44. Ibid., p. 4.
45. Jaishankar Prasad, *The Wave* (1933; rpt. Allahabad, 1969), p. 11.
46. Sahney, p. 7.
47. Ibid., p. 8.
48. Ibid.
49. Ibid., p. 5.
50. Prem Shankar, *Prasad ka Kavya* (Allahabad, 1969), p. 11.
51. Madan Gopal, *Bhartendu Harishchandra* (New Delhi, 1971), p. 7.
52. Literally, "Glory be to Shiva."

53. A wrap-around skirt.
54. Bajpai, p. 22.

Chapter Two

1. Later collected in *Chitradhar* (1918). Sahney notes that Prasad himself was not very fond of these pieces and that "it was only to please his friends that he gave his consent to their publication" (p. 11).
2. Quoted by Kishori Lal Gupta, *Prasad ka Vikasatmak Adhyayan* (Allahabad, 1971), p. 31.
3. A Banaras-based literary periodical, *Indu* published most of Prasad's early works.
4. Prasad, "Preface" to *The Pilgrim of Love* (1914; rpt. Allahabad, 1968). All subsequent citations are from this edition.
5. Ibid., p. 32.
6. Sahney, p. 12.
7. Prasad, *The Pilgrim of Love*, p. 12.
8. Ibid., p. 19.
9. Ibid., p. 32.
10. Yudhisthar was the eldest of the Pandava brothers and Duryodhan was the chief of Kauravas. The famous battle of *Mahabharata* was fought between the Pandavas and the Kauravas.
11. Gupta, p. 155.
12. The Reign of Harshavardhan, who ruled from A.D. 606 to 647, is discussed in R. K. Mookerjee, *Harsha* (London, 1926).The Chinese Buddhist pilgrim Hsuan Tsang visited India during Harsha's reign.
13. Gupta, p. 217.
14. Ibid., p. 219.
15. Prasad, *Shadow*, 2nd ed. (1918; rpt. Allahabad 1972), p. 8. All subsequent citations are from this edition.
16. Akbar (1542–1605), one of the great Moghul kings of India, makes "good the claim to be with Ashok, the two Indian statesmen of world rank before the twentieth century" (Spear, p. 38).
17. Publisher's "Preface" to Prasad, *The Waterfall*, 2nd ed. (1927; rpt. Allahabad, 1969).
18. Sahney, p. 17.
19. Generally disapproved by Muslim theologians, the Sufi saints,

Notes and References

according to Romila Thapar, attracted "sympathy and interest in India, particularly among those who were in any case inclined to mysticism" (*A History of India,* vol. 1 [London, 1966], p. 264).

20. Prasad, *The Water Fall,* p. 19.
21. Ibid., p. 60.
22. Ibid., p. 74.
23 Prem Shankar, p. 193.
24. Prasad, *The Waterfall,* p. 47.
25. Ibid., p. 28.
26 Ibid., p. 45.
27. Ibid., p. 40.
28. Ibid., p. 22.
29. Sahney, pp. 17–18.
30. Ashok (264–223 B.C.), perhaps the greatest Indian king, according to Romila Thapar, "consolidated an empire," established the communication with the outside world, and worked hard for the doctrine of *Dhamma,* which included principles of tolerance, nonviolence, and "measures associated with welfare of citizens." According to her the best-known event of his reign was his dramatic conversion to Buddhism. The destruction caused by his Kalinga Campaign filled him with remorse and Buddhism provided "the spiritual expiation" (p. 74). For detailed study of Ashok and his reign, see Romila Thapar, *Ashok and the Decline of the Mauryas* (London, 1961).
31. Prasad, *Shadow,* p. 65.
32. Ibid., p. 57.
33. The first one being Kalinga Campaign.
34. Prasad, *Shadow,* p. 67.
35. A stronghold of Rajput rulers, Chittor has traditionally been regarded as a symbol of integrity and endless resistance.
36. Shah Jahan (1592–1666), the grandson of Akbar, was, according to Spear, a Moghul emperor of great executive ability, "to which he added a love for the magnificent and a refined artistic sense" (p. 54). Best remembered for his love for his wife, whose memory the Taj Mahal commemorates, he was imprisoned by his son Aurangzeb (1618–1717). Far less tolerant than his great-grandfather and far less magnetic than his father, Aurangzeb is remembered less for his

efficiency and more for his cruelty and ruthlessness, at least by the Hindu part of the Indian subcontinent.

37. Prasad, *Shadow,* p. 77.

38. Buddhism was for a long time "a formidable rival to Hinduism" (Thapar, p. 159). Somewhat unorthodox in its approach to metaphysics, Buddhism was vehemently opposed by Hinduism for a long time. For a general historical introduction, see T. W. Rhys Davids, *Buddhism, Its History and Literature* (London, 1923). For an introduction to the confrontation between Hinduism and Buddhism see H. M. Eliot, *Hinduism and Buddhism* (London, 1922).

39. "Modern Southern Bihar," according to Thapar (p. 54).

40. Rai Krishandas, "Introduction" to Prasad *Ajatshatru* (1922; rpt. Allahabad, 1971), p. 6. All subsequent citations are from this reprint.

41. Prasad, "Preface" to *Ajatshatru,* p. 8.

42. See S. Radhakrishnan, *Indian Philosophy* (London: Allen and Unwin, 1923–27) and S . N. Das Gupta, *History of Indian Philosophy* (Cambridge, 1923–49).

43. Prasad, *Ajatshatru,* p. 29.

44. Ibid., p. 30.

45. The dance of destruction performed by Shiva.

46. Prasad, *Ajatshatru,* p. 27.

47. Ibid., p. 54.

48. Ibid., p. 107.

49. Ibid., p. 95.

50. Ibid., p. 101.

51. Ibid., p. 135.

52. Prasad, *Tears* (Jhansi, 1925). All subsequent citations in this chapter are from this edition.

53. Ibid., p. 9.

54. Ibid., p. 19.

55. Ibid.

56. Ibid., p. 27.

57. Ibid., p. 19. The translation is by Sahney, p. 12.

58. Bajpai, p. 54.

59. Sahney, p. 22.

60. From Vishwanath's "The Family," translated by J. Miles in Misra, *Modern Hindi Poetry,* pp. 76–77.

Notes and References

Chapter Three

1. Jaishankar Prasad, "Preface" to *The Nag Campaign of Janmejay* (1926; rpt. Allahabad, 1969), p. 6. All subsequent citations are from this reprint. *Nag* literally means "serpent" in Hindi. The Nag tribe apparently got its name from worshiping snakes.
2. Ibid., p. 91.
3. Ibid., p. 92.
4. Ibid., p. 34.
5. Ibid., p. 35.
6. Ibid., p. 43.
7. Gupta, *Prasad*, p. 176.
8. Ibid., p. 190.
9. Ramnath Suman, *Kavi Prasad ki Kavya Sadhana*; quoted by Gupta, *Prasad*, p. 182.
10. Jaishankar Prasad, *Kamana* (1927; rpt. Allahabad, 1968), p. 27. All subsequent citations from *Kamana* are from this reprint.
11. Ibid.
12. Ibid., p. 31.
13. Ibid., p. 43.
14. Ibid., p. 60.
15. Ibid., p. 7.
16. Ibid., p. 10.
17. Ibid., p. 24.
18. Ibid., p. 85.
19. Hardev Bahri, *Prasad Sahitya Kosh* (Allahabad, 1957), p. 348.
20. Gupta, *Prasad*, p. 162.
21. Jaishankar Prasad, *Rajyashri*, 2nd ed. (1933; rpt. Allahabad, 1956). All subsequent citations are from this reprint.
22. For a contrary view, see Gupta, *Prasad*, p. 194.
23. Ibid., p. 195.
24. Ram Ratan Bhatnagar, "History in Hindi Literature (Nonfictional)," in *History in Modern Indian Literature,* ed. S. P. Sen (Calcutta, 1975), p. 76.
25. Jaishankar Prasad, *Skandgupta*, 1928; rpt. Allahabad, 1974), p. 6. All subsequent citations from *Skandgupta* are from this reprint.
26. Ila Chand Joshi, "Skandgupta," in *Prasad Pratibha*, ed. Indra Nath Madan (Delhi, 1971), p. 100.

27. Gupta, *Prasad,* p. 185.

28. Prasad, *Skandgupta,* p. 9.

29. For a brief description of the Huna exploits in India, see Thapar, pp. 140–42.

30. On the Shaka era, see Thapar, pp. 95–98.

31. Prasad, *Skandgupta,* p. 149.

32. Action without thinking about possible rewards is the cornerstone of the ethics of *The Bhagavad Gita.*

33. Prasad, *Skandgupta,* p. 13.

34. Rajeshwara Prasad Argal, "Skandgupta," in *Prasad Pratibha,* p. 160.

35. Prasad, *Skandgupta,* p. 84.

36. Ibid., p. 136.

37. Ramchandra Shukla, *Hindi Sahitya ka Itihas* (Banaras, 1949), p. 563.

38. Gupta, *Prasad,* p. 187.

39. Prasad, *Skandgupta,* p. 144.

40. "Publisher's Preface" to Jaishankar Prasad, *One Sip* (1929; rpt. Allahabad, 1970), p. 4. All subsequent citations are from this reprint.

41. Ibid.

Chapter Four

1. Jaishankar Prasad, "The Lighthouse," in *The Lighthouse* (1929; rpt. Allahabad, 1973), p. 9. All subsequent citations are from this reprint.

2. Ibid., p. 10.

3. Ibid., p. 18.

4. Ibid.

5. Ibid., p. 19.

6. Ibid., p. 20.

7. Ibid., p. 14. Varuna is the Indian counterpart of Neptune.

8. Humayun (1508–56), the problem child of the Moghuls according to Spear, was the son of Babur and the father of Akbar. He was elegant, clever, and fascinating as well as unstable and wayward. He could, according to Spear, achieve much in a burst of energy, and then throw all away through indolence and carelessness (p. 26).

Notes and References

9. Prasad, "Mamta," in *The Lighthouse*, p. 27.
10. Ibid., p. 28.
11. Ibid., p. 30.
12. Prasad, "The Beggar Woman," in *The Lighthouse*, p. 70.
13. Prasad, "The Bangle Woman," in *The Lighthouse*, p. 131.
14. Prasad, "The Recluse," in *The Light House*, p. 114.
15. Ibid., p. 115.
16. Ibid.
17. Ibid.
18. Ibid.
19. Ibid.
20. Jaishankar Prasad, "Madhua," in *The Storm* (1929; rpt. Allahabad, 1972), p. 47. All subsequent citations from *The Storm* are from this reprint.
21. Ibid., p. 49.
22. Ibid., p. 52.
23. Prasad, "Reward," in *The Storm*, p. 143.
24. Ibid., p. 156.
25. Ibid., p. 147.
26. Prasad, "A Broken Vow," in *The Storm*, p. 99.
27. Ibid., p. 96.
28. Indra Nath Madan, "Tin Kahaniyan," in *Prasad Pratibha*, p. 236.
29. Jaishankar Prasad, *The Skeleton* (1929; rpt. Allahabad, 1972), p. 41. All subsequent citations are from this reprint.
30. Ibid., p. 57.
31. Ibid., p. 79.
32. Ganga Prasad Pandey, *"Kankal,"* in *Prasad Pratibha*, p. 203.

Chapter Five

1. Chandragupta Maurya, referred to as Sandrocottos in the Greek accounts, succeeded to the Nanda throne in 321 B.C. He was succeeded by his son Bindusar in 297 B.C. Chandragupta controlled the Indus and the Ganges plains and the far northwest.
2. Gupta, *Prasad*, p. 195.
3. Ibid.
4. Vishvambhar Manav, *"Chandragupta,"* in *Prasad Pratibha*, p. 173.
5. For the state of India at the time of Alexander's invasion, see Thapar, pp. 58–62.

6. Ambhik and Nand were both kings at the time of Alexander's invasion of India. The Nandas, according to Thapar, were "the first empire builders of India" (p. 57).

7. Taxila was the center of both education and commerce at the time of Alexander's invasion. Situated in northern India, it was the capital of Gandhara.

8. Apparently a historical fact.

9. Seleucus Nikator.

10. Jaishankar Prasad, *Chandragupta* (1931; rpt. Delhi, 1974), p. 156. All subsequent citations are from this reprint.

11. Ibid.

12. Ibid., p. 48.

13. Ibid., p. 46.

14. Ibid., p. 64.

15. Ibid., p. 61.

16. Manav, p. 176.

17. Prasad, *Chandragupta*, p. 62.

18. Ibid., p. 45.

19. Ibid., p. 101.

20. Ibid., p. 118.

21. Jaishankar Prasad, "Preface" to *Dhruvaswamini* (1933; rpt. Allahabad, 1971), pp. vii–ix. All subsequent citations are from this reprint.

22. Ibid., p. x.

23. Prasad, *Dhruwaswamini*, p. 27.

24. Ibid.

25. Ibid.

26. Shambhu Prasad Bahuguna, *"Dhruvaswamini,"* in *Prasad Pratibha*, p. 124.

Chapter Six

1. Jaishankar Prasad, *Tears*, 2nd ed. (1933; rpt. Allahabad, 1969), p. 49. All subsequent citations are from this reprint. Citations from the first edition are identified as such in the text.

2. Ibid., p. 15.

3. Ramesh Chandra Shah, "Giti Shrasti," in *Prasad Pratibha*, p. 10.

4. Prasad, *Tears*, p. 1.

5. Ibid., p. 19.

Notes and References

6. Ibid., p. 21.
7. Jayasi was a mystic poet in the Sufi tradition.
8. Prasad, *Tears*, p. 21.
9. Ibid., p. 58.
10. Ibid., p. 79.
11. The form made famous by Omar Khayyam.
12. Bajpai, p. 57.
13. Prasad, *Tears*, p. 17.
14. Ibid., p. 10.
15. Jaishankar Prasad, *The Wave* (1933; rpt. Allahabad, 1969), p. 11. All subsequent citations from *The Wave* are from this reprint.
16. Ibid., p. 36.
17. Ibid., p. 9.
18. Ibid., p. 45.
19. Ibid., p. 14.
20. Sahney, p. 25.
21. Prasad, *The Wave*, p. 39.
22. Sahney, p. 25.
23. *Titali* literally means "butterfly" in Hindi.
24. Padam Singh Sharma Kamlesh, *"Titali,"* in *Prasad Pratibha*, p. 237.

Chapter Seven

1. For a similar view, see Gupta, *Prasad*.
2. Jaishankar Prasad, *Kamayani*, tr. Jaikishandas Sadani (Calcutta, 1975), p. 3. All subsequent citations from *Kamayani* are, unless indicated otherwise, from this translation.
3. Ibid.
4. Ibid.
5. Ibid., p. 19.
6. Ibid., p. 25.
7. Shradha and Kamayani both refer to the same person, *Kamayani* literally means "the daughter of Kama, the Indian god of love." *Shradha* etymologically means "the preserver and purveyor of truth." Kama, it must be remembered, denotes something more than a mere libido sense. Lodha in his introduction to Sadani's translation of *Kamayani* observes, "As Vincent Smith has rightly pointed out, it is Kama that bears a combined meaning of the Libido and the Eros of

the Greek mythology. It is the basic urge of life—the creative urge and instinct; the sense to preserve, protect and expand. In Vedic hymns, it has been praised as an all-pervading consciousness and the root of life" (p.iii).
8. A pillarlike structure.
9. Prasad, *Kamayani*, p. 38.
10. See note 3 above.
11. Prasad, *Kamayani*, p. 57.
12. Ibid., p. 77.
13. Ibid., p. 87.
14. A sort of racial unconscious.
15. Prasad, *Kamayani*, p. 95.
16. Ibid., p. 110.
17. Ibid., p. 123.
18. Ibid., p. 124.
19. Ibid.
20. *Ida* is translated by Sadani as "intelligence."
21. Prasad, *Kamayani*, p. 142.
22. Tandav is Shiva's dance of destruction.
23. Prasad, *Kamayani*, p. 158.
24. Ibid., p. 167.
25. Ibid., p. 171.
26. Ibid., p. 181.
27. Ibid., p. 201.
28. Ibid., p. 202.
29. Ibid., p. 207.
30. Ibid., p. 219.
31. Ibid., p. 234.
32. Ibid.
33. Ibid., p. 251.
34. Prasad, "Preface" to *Kamayani*, p. xi.
35. Ibid., p. viii.
36. Lodha, p. iv.
37. Matsyendra Shukla, *Jaishankar Prasad: Jivan aur Sahitya* (Allahabad, 1971), p. 97.
38. *Manav* literally means "man."
39. Prasad, *Kamayani*, p. 138.
40. Ibid., p. 36.

Notes and References

41. Ibid.
42. Ibid., p. 4.
43. Ibid., p. 5.
44. Ibid., p. 11.
45. Ibid., p. 13.
46. The Indian goddess of Dawn.
47. The Indian goddess of wealth.
48. Prasad, *Kamayani,* p. 19.
49. Ibid.
50. The favorite drink of Indian gods.
51. Prasad, *Kamayani,* p. 20.
52. Ibid., p. 11.
53. A tropical tree, commonly associated with the sensual adventures of Krishna.
54. Prasad, *Kamayani,* p. 77.
55. Ibid., p. 85.
56. Ibid., p. 5.
57. P. Lal, one of the best-known translators of Indian literature, has this to say in his foreword to Sadani's translation of *Kamayani*: "Because Kamayani is so permeated with Hindu myth, I think it is one of the most difficult books to get successfully across into English. A new idiom has to be constructed to convey the subtleties" (p. vii).
58. Ramlal Singh, *Kamayani Anushilan* (Allahabad, 1959), p. 103.
59. Ramesh Chandra Gupta, *Kamayani ki Bhasha* (Delhi, 1964), pp. 90ff.
60. Ibid., p. 126.
61. Namvar Singh, "Bhasha-Shaili," in *Prasad Pratibha,* pp. 241–51.
62. Mahavir Prasad Dwivedi, *Rasagya Ranjan,* 2nd ed. (1900: rpt. Agra, 1949), p. 18.
63. The device is used frequently by Cummings.
64. Prasad, *Kamayani,* p. 110.
65. Lal, p. viii.
66. Gajanand Madhav Muktibodh, *Kamayani: Ek Punarvichar* (Delhi: National Publishing House, 1970), p. 21.
67. Ibid., p. 123.
68. Prasad, *Kamayani,* p. 210.
69. Ibid., p. 3.
70. Ibid., p. 251.

71. Ibid., p. 248.
72. Lal, p. viii.
73. Sahney, p. 27.
74. Ibid., p. 28.
75. Suresh Gautam, *Kamayani: Ek Utopia* (Delhi: Rajesh Prakashan, 1978:), p. 53.

Chapter Eight

1. Jaishankar Prasad, "Gangster," in *The Web* (1936; rpt. Allahabad, 1969), p. 84. All subsequent citations from *The Web* are from this reprint.
2. Prasad, *The Web*, p. 107.
3. Ibid., p. 55.
4. Ibid., p. 38.
5 Prasad, "Comma," in *The Web*, p. 113.
6. Jaishankar Prasad, *Iravati* (1937; rpt. Allahabad, 1967), p. 15. All subsequent citations are from this reprint.
7. Ibid., p. 13.
8. Ibid., p. 14.
9. Ibid., p. 4.
10. Ibid., p. 19.
11. Ibid., p. 70.
12. Jaishankar Prasad, *Poetry and Art and Other Essays* (1937; rpt. Allahabad, 1969), p. 30. All subsequent citations are from this reprint.
13. Ibid., p. 29.
14. Ibid., p. 68.
15. Ibid., p. 125.
16. Ibid.
17. Ibid., p. 87.
18. Ibid., p. 107.
19. Ratna Shankar Prasad, "Introduction" to *The Music of Prasad* (Allahabad: Bharati Bhandar, 1956), p. 1.
20. Ibid., p. 88
21. An obvious reference to the promise made to Arjun by Krishna. S. Radhaknishnan renders the relevant lines thus in his translation of *The Bhagavad Gita* (2nd ed., London: Blackie and Son, 1949):

Whenever righteousness declines, O Bharata
And unrighteousness uprises, then I create thyself

Notes and References

> For the protection of the good and destruction of the
> wicked, and to
> Confirm the right I am born from age to age. (4:7–8)

22. Ratna Shankar Prasad. ed., *The Music of Prasad*, p. 85.
23. Ibid., p. 1.
24. Ibid., p. 10.
25. Ibid., p. 107.
26. Ibid., p. 92.
27. Ibid., p. 91.
28. Ibid., p. 2.
29. Ibid., p. 49.
30. The divine poems of John Donne can be regarded as falling within these categories.
31. Ratna Shankar Prasad, ed., *The Music of Prasad*, p. 94.
32. Ibid., p. 82.
33. Ramsaran, p. 163.
34. Ratna Shankar Prasad, ed., *The Music of Prasad*, p. 7.
35. Ibid.. p. 97.

Chapter Nine

1. For this view of science, see Thomas S. Kuhn, *The Structure of Scientific Revolutions* (Chicago: University of Chicago, 1962).
2. Prasad, *Dhruwaswamini*, p. 10.
3. Bhatnagar, p. 77.
4. Reported by Sharma, p. 276.

Selected Bibliography

PRIMARY SOURCES

Shadow [*Chaya*]. 1912; rpt. Allahabad: Bharati Bhandar, 1968.
Flowers of the Garden [*Kanan Kusum*]. 1912; rpt. Allahabad: Bharati Bhandar, 1966.
The Pilgrim of Love [*Prem-Pathik*]. 1914; rpt. Allahabad: Bharati Bhandar, 1968.
Rajyashri. Banaras: Indu, 1915.
Chitradhar. Banaras: Hindi Pustak Mala, 1918.
The Waterfall [*Jharana*]. 1918; rpt. Allahabad: Bharati Bhandar, 1969.
Vishakha. Banaras: Hindi Granth Bhandar, 1921.
Ajatshatru. 1922; rpt. Allahabad: Bharati Bhandar, 1971.
Tears [*Ansoo*]. Jhansi: Sahitya Sadan, 1925.
The Nag Campaign of Janmejay [*Janmejay ka Nagyagya*]. 1926; rpt. Allahabad: Bharati Bhandar, 1969.
Echo [*Pratidhwani*]. 1926; rpt. Allahabad: Bharati Bhandar, 1969.
Kamana, 1927; rpt. Allahabad: Bharati Bhandar, 1968.
The House of Pity [*Karunalay*]. 1928; rpt. Allahabad: Bharati Bhandar, 1961.
Skandgupta. 1928; rpt. Allahabad: Bharati Bhandar, 1974.
The Lighthouse [*Akash Deep*]. 1929; rpt. Allahabad: Bharati Bhandar, 1973.
The Skeleton [*Kankal*]. 1929; rpt. Allahabad: Bharati Bhandar, 1972.
One Sip [*Ek Ghunt*]. 1929; rpt. Allahabad: Bharati Bhandar, 1970.
The Storm [*Andhi*]. 1929; rpt. Allahabad: Bharati Bhandar, 1972.
Chandragupta. 1931; rpt. Delhi: Prasad Prakashan, 1974.
Tears [*Ansoo*]. 2nd ed., 1933; rpt. Allahabad: Bharati Bhandar, 1969.
Dhruwaswamini. 1933; rpt. Allahabad: Bharati Bhandar, 1971.
The Wave [*Lahar*]. 1933; rpt. Allahabad: Bharati Bhandar, 1969.
Kamayani. 1935; rpt. Allahabad: Bharati Bhandar, 1969.
The Web [*Indrajal*]. 1936; rpt. Allahabad: Bharati Bhandar, 1969.
Iravati. 1937; rpt. Allahabad: Bharati Bhandar, 1967.

Selected Bibliography

Poetry and Art and Other Essays [*Kavya aur Kala tatha anya Nibandh*]. 1937; rpt. Allahabad: Bharati Bhandar, 1969.

TRANSLATIONS

Kamayani. Translated by B. L. Sahney. New Delhi: Yugbodh, 1971.
Kamayani. Translated by Jaikishan Das Sadani. Calcutta: Rupa and Co., 1975.

SECONDARY SOURCES

BAHARI, HARDEV. *Prasad Sahitya Kosh*. Allahabad: Bharati Bhandar, 1957. A dictionary of Prasadian literature, it is one of the most useful works on Prasad.

BAJPAI, NAND DULARE. *Jaishankar Prasad*. Allahabad: Bharati Bhandar, 1966. A collection of critical essays by one of the best classical critics of Hindi.

BHATNAGAR, RAM RATNA. *Prasad ki Vichar Dhara*. Allahabad: Ramnarain Lal, n.d. Though it contains some useful information, particularly regarding publication dates of Prasad's works, it is a rather discursive critical evaluation of the author.

———. "History in Hindi Literature (Non-fictional)." In *History in Modern Indian Literature*. Edited by S. P. Sen. Calcutta: Institute of Historical Studies, 1975. pp. 72–82. A perceptive discussion of the treatment of Indian history in Hindi literature.

BHATT, SOMNATH. *Hindi Sahitya ka Itihas Digdarshan*. Poona: Venus Prakashan, 1965. A good brief history of Hindi literature.

BHATTACHARYA, JOGENDRA NATH. *Hindu Castes and Sects*. Calcutta: Thacker, 1896. An intelligent and useful discussion of the Indian caste system, the knowledge of which is essential for understanding Prasad's historical plays.

CUMMINGS, JOHN, ed. *Political India: 1832–1932*. London: O.U.P., 1932. Provides extremely useful background for the hundred years covered by it.

DAS GUPTA, S. N. *History of Indian Philosophy*. Cambridge: Cambridge University Press, 1923–49. Some knowledge of Indian philosophy is essential for understanding Prasad's philosophical concerns. This book provides an authentic historical outline of those concerns.

DWIVEDI, MAHAVIR PRASAD. *Rasgya Ranjan.* 2nd ed., 1900; rpt. Agra: Sahitya Ratna Bhandar, 1949. The poetics by the guru of the neo-classicism Prasad reacted against.

DWIVEDI, RAM AWADH. *A Critical Survey of Hindi Literature.* Banaras: Motilal Banarasidas, 1966. A brief, but good, survey of Hindi literature.

ELIOT, H. M. *Hinduism and Buddhism.* London: Edwin Arnold, 1922. A good general account of the conflict between Hinduism and Buddhism, which plays a central role in so many of Prasad's works.

GOPAL, MADAN. *Bhartendu Harischandra.* New Delhi: Sahitya Akademi, 1971. Provides extremely useful information regarding the literary climate of Prasad's formative years.

GUPTA, KISHORI LAL. *Prasad ka Vikasatmak Adhyayan.* Allahabad: Rachna Prakashan, 1971. Although it does not contain much perceptive criticism, it provides authentic information regarding dates of publication, editions, and reprints. Absolutely essential.

GUPTA, RAMESH CHANDRA. *Kamayani ki Bhasha.* Delhi: Ashok Prakashan, 1964. Originally written as a master's thesis for the University of Delhi, it examines the language of Kamayani according to the general principles of classical Indian rhetoric.

JINDAL, K. B. *A History of Hindi Literature.* Allahabad: Kitab Mahal, 1955. One of the very few histories of Hindi literature in English.

MADAN, INDRANATH, ed. *Prasad Pratibha.* Delhi: National Publishing House, 1971. A collection of some of the best recent critical studies of Prasad's individual works.

MCGREGOR, RONALD STUART. *Hindi Literature of the Nineteenth and Early Twentieth Centuries.* Wiesbaden: Otto Harrassowitz, 1974. An excellent introduction to the literature of the age immediately before that of Prasad.

MISHRA, JAGDISH PRASAD. *Shakespeare's Impact on Hindi Literature.* New Delhi: Munshiram Manohar Lal, 1970. Originally a doctoral dissertation, this study, though an example of comparative literature at its worst, provides some useful information regarding the history and development of Hindi theater.

Selected Bibliography

MOOKERJEE, R. K. *Harsha*. London: Oxford University Press, 1926. Provides a brief but illuminating account of Harsha and his reign.

RAI, GULAB. *Hindi Sahitya ka Subodh Itihas*. Agra: Mahendra Prakashan, 1975. Provides a quick survey of Hindi literature.

RAMSARAN, JOHN A. *English and Hindi Religious Poetry: An Anological Study*. Leiden: E. J. Brill, 1973. A comparative study of English Metaphysical and Hindi Bhakti poets, it seeks to substantiate the hypothesis that *Bhakti* is a recurrent aspect of universal poetry. It is a good introduction to a cross-linguistic understanding of religious poetry.

RHYS DAVIDS, T. W. *Buddhism, Its History and Literature*. London: G. P. Putnam, 1923. An excellent general introduction to the history and literature of Buddhism.

RUBIN, DAVID. *Selected Poems of Nirala*. New York: Columbia University Press, 1976. Contains some very good translations and a perceptive account of the poetry of Nirala, Prasad's friend and contemporary.

SADIQ, MUHAMMED. *A History of Urdu Literature*. London: Oxford University Press, 1964. One of the very few histories of the literature in "the other" dialect of Hindustani.

SEN, K. M. *Medieval Mysticism in India*. London: Oxford University Press, 1936. An extremely useful account of the growth of mysticism in medieval India.

SHANKAR, PREM. *Prasad ka Kavya*. Allahabad: Bharati Bhandar, 1969. A good, though somewhat orthodox, discussion of Prasad's poetry.

SHARMA, JAGANNATH PRASAD. *Prasad ke Natakon ka Shashtriya Adhyayan*. Banaras: Sarswati Mandir, 1943. An orthodox critical examination of Prasad's plays according to the general principles of classical Indian dramaturgy.

SHARMA, RAJMANI. "Prasad ka Gadya Sahitya." Diss. Banaras Hindu University 1975. The only detailed evaluation of Prasad's prose.

SHARMA, SHRI RAM. *The Arya Samaj and Its Impact on Contemporary India*. Una: Institute of Public Administration, n.d. Provides useful discussion of one of the major "reform" movements of Prasad's India.

SHASHTRI, RAM AWADH. *Kamayani Sarveksna*. Banaras: Vishwa Vidyalay Prakashan, 1970. Essentially a rather mediocre commentary on

Kamayani, it contains a useful discussion of the development of Prasad's literary career.

SHUKLA, RAMCHANDRA. *Hindi Sahitya ka Itihas*. Banaras: Nagari Pracharni Sabha, 1949. One of the first histories of Hindi literature, it is still something of a classic.

SHUKLA, MATSYENDRA. *Jaishankar Prasad: Jivan aur Sahitya*. Allahabad: Smriti Prakashan, 1971. A running commentary on Prasad's works, generously punctuated with textual quotations.

SINGH, NAMWAR. "Hindi." In *Indian Literature Since Independence*. Edited by K. R. Srinivas Iyenger. New Delhi: Sahitya Akademi, 1973, pp. 79–92. An informative and perceptive discussion of post-Prasadian Hindi literature by one of Hindi's more enlightened critics.

SINGH, RAMLAL. *Kamayani Anushilan*. Allahabad: Indian Press, 1959. An early sympathetic evaluation of *Kamayani*.

SPEAR, PERCIVAL. *A History of India: Vol. 2*. London: Penguin, 1965. A very readable and informative discussion of relatively recent Indian history.

SUMAN, RAMNATH. *Kavi Prasad ki Kavya Sadhana*. Allahabad: Bharati Bhandar, 1960. A good traditional survey of Prasad's poetry.

SWAN, ROBERT O. *Munshi Premchand of Lamhi Village*. Durham, N.C.: Duke University Press, 1969. An extremely useful, though somewhat unorganized, study of the sociopolitical climate of Prasad's India.

THAPAR, ROMILA. *Ashok and the Decline of the Mauryas*. London: Oxford University Press, 1961. A must for an understanding of Ashok's India.

———. *A History of India: Vol. 1*. London: Penguin, 1966. A first-rate introduction to India's somewhat obscure past by one of India's leading younger historians.

VARMA, DHIRENDRA, *La Langue Braj*. Paris: Adrien Maisonneuve, 1937. Although a technical linguistic description of Braj, the book provides some useful information regarding the history of Braj and Standard Hindi, the dialect finally chosen by Prasad.

VATSYAYAN, S. H. "Hindi Literature." In *Contemporary Indian Literature: A Symposium*. New Delhi: Sahitya Akademi, 1957, pp. 78–99. An extremely perceptive survey of modern Hindi literature by one of Hindi's best-known contemporary poets (pseudonymn Agyeya).

Index

"Action" ["Karma"], 90
Akbar, 21, 107
Alexander, 24, 68
"Anniversary of Shri Krishna" ["Shri Krishna Jayanti"], 18
Anonymous [*Anamika*] (Nirala), 8
"Anxiety" ["Chinta"], 88
Arthashastra (Chanakya), 68
Aristotle, 14
Arnold, Matthew, 14
Ashoka, 24, 129n30
"Ashoka," 24
"Ashoka's Worry," 83
Aurangzeb, 25–26
"Autobiography" ["Atma Katha"], 13

Bahri, Hardev, 44
Bai, Sideshwari, 14
Bajpai, Nand Dulare, 13, 33
Banaras, 11, 14–16
"Bangle Woman, The" ["Churiwali"], 56
Bardai, Chand, 1
"Bashfulness" ["Lajja"], 89
"Beggar Woman" ["Bhikarin"], 55
"Beginnings of Drama" ["Natakon ka Arambh"], 113
"Beloved" ["Priyatam"], 23
Bengali, 14

Bhagavad Gita, 47
bhajans, 116
Bhakti, 1, 5, 7–9, 33, 116
Bhatnager, Ram Ratna, 45
Bihari, 5
"Bliss" ["Anand"], 93
Brahmanism, 37, 38, 108
Braj, 17, 18
"Brave Child" ["Vir Balak"], 18
Buddha, 28, 29
Buddhism, 28, 30, 40, 73, 106, 108
"Broken Vow, A" ["Vrat Bhang"], 61, 63

"Chain" ["Bedi"], 63
Chand, Jay, 19
"Chariot of the Gods, The" ["Deva-ratha"], 106
Chand, Prem, 11, 16, 74, 122, 123
Chandragupta, 68, 133n1
Chhayavad, 7–11, 21, 111–13, 121
Christianity, 107
"Comma" ["Viram Chinha"], 107
"Command" ["Adesh"], 22

"Desire" ["Kama"], 89
Divine Comedy (Dante), 14, 104
"Doubt" ["Sandeh"], 106–107

145

"Dream" ["Swapna"], 91
"Dreamland" ["Swapna-lok], 23
Dwivedi, Pandit Mahavir Prasad, 6, 100

"Echo" ["Pratidhwani"], 56
Embree, Ainslie, 3
English, 14
"Envy" ["Irshya"], 90

Faerie Queen, The (Edmund Spencer), 104
Friend, Corinne, 5
Frost [*Nihar*] (Mahadevi Varma), 8

Gandhi, Mahatma, 10, 74
Ganges, 15
"Gangster" ["Gunda"], 105, 107
Gautam, Suresh, 104
Gift of a Cow, The (Prem Chand), 122
Gopal, Madan, 14
Gupta, Ramesh Chandra, 99
Gupta empire, 46

Harishchandra Magazine, 16
Harshavardhan, 19
Heroic Age, 1
Hindi: language, 86, 102; literature, 1, 6, 14, 107, 110, 112, 119
Hinduism, 2, 3, 10, 15, 30, 107
Homer, 14
"Hope" ["Asha"], 88
"How Hard is the Flame of Youth," 115

In Memoriam (Alfred Lord Tennyson), 33

"India" ["Bharat"], 18
Indu, 18, 115
Islam, 2, 107

"Jahanara," 25
Jainism, 28, 107
Jayasi, 9

Kabir, 2, 9
Khari Boli, 1, 6, 17, 18
Krishandas, Rai, 27

Lal, P., 103
Leaves [*Pallav*] (Sumitrenandan Pant), 8
"Liberation of Chittor, The" ["Chittor Uddhar"], 25
"Lighthouse, The" ["Akash Deep"], 51, 53–54, 60

MacBeth (Shakespeare), 19
McGregor, Ronald Stuart, 6
mahakavya, 86
"Madhua," 59, 63
Mahabharat, 35, 47
"Mamata," 54
mantras, 117
Milton, John, 14
Modern Age, 1, 7, 9
"Moon, the" ["Chanda"], 20
Muktibodh, Gajanand Madhav, 102
Mysticism, *see* Rahasyavad

Nagari Pracharini Sabha, 16
"Nightingale Sings in the Garden of Youth Today, The," 115
Nirala, 8, 122
"Nuri," 107

Index

"Oath of Alexander, The" ["Sikandar Ki Shapatha"], 24
"Oh Youth Your Unstable Shadow," 116

"Painted Rocks" ["Chitravale Patthar"], 107
Pal, Sushma, 8
Pant, Sumitrenandan, 8
Parasi, 121
"Passion" ["Vasana"], 89, 100
Persian, 14
Plato, 14
Poet's Voice [*Kavi Vachan Sudha*], 16
"Poetry and Art" ["Kavya aur Kala"], 111
Prasad, Jaishankar: first practitioner of Chhayavad, 8; sociopolitical context, 10; biographical data, 11–14, on the individual and tradition, 38; on Reason and Faith, 95, 98

WORKS: DRAMA
Ajashatru, 27–30, 35–36, 40, 45, 48, 73, 101
Chandragupta, 13, 20, 21, 25, 51, 67, 68–73, 117, 120
Dhruwaswamini, 20, 25, 62, 74–76, 100, 120, 121
Gentleman [*Sajjan*], 19, 44
Kamana, 40
Nag Campaign of Janmejay, The, 35–36, 40
One Sip [*Ek Ghunt*], 49–50, 101
Penance [*Prayshchit*], 19, 44
Rajyashri, 19–20, 36, 44, 107
Skandgupta, 13, 20, 25, 45–51, 101, 117, 120, 121, 123

Vishakha, 26–28, 35, 74

WORKS: POETRY
Flowers of the Garden [*Kanan Kusum*], 17, 115
House of Pity, The, 115
Kamayani, 44, 86–88, 93–104, 118, 122
Music of Prasad [*Prasad Sangit*], 115, 118
Pilgrim of Love, The [*Prem Pathika*], 18, 19
Tears [*Ansoo*], 31–35, 45, 77–78, 81, 101, 122, 123
Waterfall, The [*Jharana*], 8, 19, 21–23, 115, 122
Wave, The [*Lahar*], 81–83, 115, 122

WORKS: PROSE
Iravati, 21, 105, *108–110*, 115
Lighthouse, The [*Akash Deep*], 51–53, 56–57
Poetry and Art and Other Essays [*Kavya aur Kala tatha Anya Nibandh*], 105, 111
Shadow [*Chhaya*], 20, 24, 25
Skeleton, The [*Kankal*], 51, 56, 64–66, 83–85
Storm, The [*Andhi*], 51
Titali, 83–85, 110
Web, The [*Indrajal*], 105, 107
Prasad, Ratna Shankar, 115
prathanas, 116

Rahasyavad, 111–12
Ramayana (Tulsidas), 3
Ramsaran, John A., 117
rasa, 2, 113, 125n3
"Rasa," 113

Realism, *see* Yartathavad
"Recluse, The" ["Vairagi"], 57, 59
"Renunciation" ["Nirveda"], 91
Republic (Plato), 104
"Request" ["Nivedan"], 23
"Revelation" [Darshan"], 91
"Reward" ["Puruskar"], 60, 63
Romanticism, *see* Chhayavad
Rossetti, Dante Gabriel, 14

Saga of Prithvi Raj, The (Chand Bardai), 1
Sahney, B. L., 13–14, 21, 23, 83, 104
Samrasa, 14, 94
Sanskrit, 12, 14, 119
Sarasvati, 6
Sarasvati, Swami Dayanand, 10
Satsai (Bihari), 5
"Salvati," 107
"Sculptural Beauty" ["Shilpa-Saundarya"], 18
"Secret" "Rahasya," 92
"Shadow of Destruction, The" ["Prayala Ki Chhaya"], 83
Shahjahan, 25, 112, 129n36
Shakespeare, 19
Shanti, 16
Shelley, Percy Bysshe, 14
Shiva, 16
Singh, Ramlal, 99
Sophocles, 14
Sorrows of Young Werther, The (Goethe), 33

"Stage" ["Rangamanch"], 91
"Struggle 2" ["Sangharsh"], 91
Sudha, 16

tandava, 29
"Tansen," 20
Thucydides, 14
"To Neglect" ["Upeksa Karana"], 23
Tulsidas, 2, 5

Ucchavas (Sumitrenandan Pant), 8
"Undying Memory" ["Amit Smriti"], 63
Urdu, 14
"Uses of Rasa in Drama" ["Natakon me Rasa Ka Prayog"], 113
Utopia (Thomas More), 104

Varanasi, *see* Banaras
Varma, Mahadevi, 8, 9, 122
"Village" ["Gram"], 20
"Village Song, The" [Gram-Geet"], 63
Vishwanath, 33

"Waiting for Spring" ["Vasant ki Pratiksa"], 23
"When" ["Kab"], 23
Wordsworth, William, 14

Yatarthavad, 112

Zoroastrianism, 107

THE LIBRARY
ST. MARY'S COLLEGE OF MARYLAND
ST. MARY'S CITY, MARYLAND 20686